MW00784781

CONTENTS

INTRODUCTION

The Pit Boss Wood Pellet Grill

The History of The Pit Boss

Founded in 1999, Pit Boss produces a wide range of grilling equipment, including charcoal and gas grills. But it's best known for pellet grills. Pit Boss focuses on affordability and simplicity, often choosing to forgo the latest technological upgrades. However, it still remains relevant. In fact, it began incorporating remote settings using Bluetooth on its Platinum line of grills in 2020.Where are Pit Boss grills made? Pit Boss is a subsidiary of Dansons Inc., which also makes Louisiana Grills. It manufactures Pit Boss in China.

Why Pit Boss Wood Pellet Stands Out From The Rest

Many wood pellet brands, including pit boss, comes with its features. Here's where pit boss pellet grills stand out.

Price

Price is a crucial factor everyone considers when shopping for any product. Of course, we all want an excellent product, but within our budget range. Most pit boss grills cost less than a thousand bucks. Pit boss ensures that most of its pellet grills fall between the $500-$700 price ranges. That's pretty affordable compared to other brands with similar features.

Construction

As much as price is important, construction is super-important. No matter how much or less you spend on a pellet grill; you will want it to last for several years. In terms of design and construction, I've never seen a brand as good as a pit boss. Most pit boss pellet grills are designed with non-toxic coating and cast iron grates.

How to Start a Pit Boss Wood Pellet Grill?

There are some steps that you can take to start the Pit Boss Pellet Grill so that it grills the steak to perfection. If you follow the guidelines below, you will have a delicious meal whose taste you will remember all week long.

Fill the Grill Up with Fuel

The step that you need to take is to make sure that you double-check whether you have more than enough pellets in the Pit Boss Pellet Grill. If the pellets are too less, it will mess up the temperature of the grill. This will result in a subpar steak at best. A good rule of thumb to follow is to have at least 2 lbs. of pellets on hand for every hour of smoking for a slow and low cook. If you want to grill hot and fast, you will have to stock up on 4 lbs. of pellets. There are different types of pellets that will give your steak different tastes. It all depends on what you want as the end result. Some of the most popular types of pellets include Hardwood, Black Cherry, and Hickory wood pellets.

Set the Grill on Smoke

Once you have made sure that you are fueled up, it is now time to set the grill on the 'smoke' option. This is a very important step on the way to getting the perfect steak because the grill will begin to feed the pellets for around 3 ½ to 4 minutes. It will then stop so that you have the chance to light up the grill before feeding the grill with more fuel. However, if you turn up the grill and set it to around 400°F, the grill will fill up the Pit Boss Pellet Grill until it reaches the temperature you have set. You will have to make sure that there isn't too much fuel over the igniter or else the grill will begin to muffle. This will probably result in it never lighting up and you having to clean it out before you can use it again. If you don't clear out the pellets that have piled up on the hopper, they will eventually begin to spill all over the place.

Start to Prep the Food

Pit Boss Pellet Grills are known to light up fairly quickly. You will have around 3 minutes to turn the grill on from the time you have it up. This is why it important to have all your meat seasoned and prepared for the grill beforehand. If you take too long, it will also impact the cooking time.

Watch Out for the Smoke

You need to look out for the thick smoky clouds coming out of the grill. This will let you know if the grill is on the right track or not. If you see thick clouds of smoke, it means that your pot has caught on fire and your pellets have begun to burn up. The smoke is often robust and full, so there is no need to be alarmed if you notice the thick smoke. The smoke tends to billow out of the grill for around 3-4 minutes before dissipating. Once the smoke has dissipated, you can start the grilling process.

Time to Start Grilling

Once the pot catches, you will hear the unmistakable sizzle and crackle from the fire. The roaring sound of the fire is the result of the fan blowing on the fire inside the grill. Now, it is time to crank up the temperature to a suitable heat and get started with the grilling process. Within 5-6 minutes, the heat will climb up to the temperature you want, and you can slap the steak right on there for the best meal of your life.

Tips on Using Your Pit Boss Wood Pellet Grill

Did you just get your Grill? I've been using mine Grill now for about a month and I have 5 beginner tips to help you off to a great start. Do you have any tips to share? Please let us know down in the comments. Clean your Pit Boss smoker while it is still warm instead of the next day or the next time you decide to smoke something.

Use your Water Pan. So many good reasons to do so... I give you two.

Invest in a good external meat probe. The pit temperature you see on the display is next to the burn pot and fluctuates as new pellets get pushed in. Its more important to monitor the temp at the rack level where your meat is. Putting your meat into the Pit Boss Pellet Smoker cold helps you get a better smoke ring. Know your pellets. Learn to pair the right kinds of pellets with the right kinds of meats/ fish/vegetables.

Best Pit Boss Pellet Grills (FAQs)

Why should I buy Pit Boss Pellet Grill?

Pit boss is a company that is oriented at designing the best grilling and smoking units that can solve all your cooking and grilling problems. Many customers have trusted them in producing high-quality pellet grills that are more effective, efficient and convenient to use.

Why are Pit Boss Pellet Grills different from others?

Pit Boss Pellet grills have copper-finished lids, and some models come with auxiliaries like a flame boiler and bottle opener. These pellet grills use natural hardwood pellets and come with an on board digital control and monitoring with a LED readout. Their meat probe and digital temp control features make them stand out among on most of the competition.

How does the pellet electric ignition work?

Pellet auger picks up the wood pellets from the grill hopper and takes them to the fire pot. The electronic ignition heats the pellets and starts the grill fire.

What can I cook on my pit boss pellet grill?

A lot of things. With a pit boss grill, you can cook a pizza, sear a steak, smoke a brisket, or even bake chocolate chip cookies. Their large cooking area and full precise temperature control allow this to happen.

FISH AND SEAFOOD RECIPES

1.   Wine Infused Salmon

Servings: 4
Cooking Time: 5 Hours
Ingredients:
- 2 C. low-sodium soy sauce
- 1 C. dry white wine
- 1 C. water
- ½ tsp. Tabasco sauce
- 1/3 C. sugar
- ¼ C. salt
- ½ tsp. garlic powder
- ½ tsp. onion powder
- Freshly ground black pepper, to taste
- 4 (6-oz.) salmon fillets

Directions:
1. In a large bowl, add all ingredients except salmon and stir until sugar is dissolved.
2. Add salmon fillets and coat with brine well.
3. Refrigerate, covered overnight.
4. Remove salmon from bowl and rinse under cold running water.
5. With paper towels, pat dry the salmon fillets.
6. Arrange a wire rack in a sheet pan.
7. Place the salmon fillets onto wire rack, skin side down and set aside to cool for about 1 hour.
8. Set the temperature of Grill to 165 degrees F and preheat with closed lid for 15 minutes, using charcoal.
9. Place the salmon fillets onto the grill, skin side down and cook for about 3-5 hours or until desired doneness.
10. Remove the salmon fillets from grill and serve hot.

Nutrition Info: Calories per serving: 377; Carbohydrates: 26.3g; Protein: 41.1g; Fat: 10.5g; Sugar: 25.1g; Sodium: 14000mg; Fiber: 0g

2.   Salmon With Togarashi

Servings: 3
Cooking Time: 20 Minutes
Ingredients:
- 1 salmon fillet
- 1/4 cup olive oil
- 1/2 tbsp kosher salt
- 1 tbsp Togarashi seasoning

Directions:
1. Preheat your to 400F.
2. Place the salmon on a sheet lined with non-stick foil with the skin side down.
3. Rub the oil into the meat then sprinkle salt and Togarashi.
4. Place the salmon on the grill and cook for 20 minutes or until the internal temperature reaches 145F with the lid closed.
5. Remove from the and serve when hot.

Nutrition Info: Calories 119, Total fat 10g, Saturated fat 2g, Total carbs 0g, Net carbs 0g Protein 0g, Sugars 0g, Fiber 0g, Sodium 720mg

3.   Enticing Mahi-mahi

Servings: 4
Cooking Time: 10 Minutes
Ingredients:
- 4 (6-oz.) mahi-mahi fillets
- 2 tbsp. olive oil
- Salt and freshly ground black pepper, to taste

Directions:
1. Set the temperature of Grill to 350 degrees F and preheat with closed lid for 15 minutes.
2. Coat fish fillets with olive oil and season with salt and black pepper evenly.
3. Place the fish fillets onto the grill and cook for about 5 minutes per side.
4. Remove the fish fillets from grill and serve hot.

Nutrition Info: Calories per serving: 195; Carbohydrates: 0g; Protein: 31.6g; Fat: 7g; Sugar: 0g; Sodium: 182mg; Fiber: 0g

4.   Crazy Delicious Lobster Tails

Servings: 4
Cooking Time: 25 Minutes
Ingredients:
- ½ C. butter, melted
- 2 garlic cloves, minced
- 2 tsp. fresh lemon juice
- Salt and freshly ground black pepper, to taste
- 4 (8-oz.) lobster tails

Directions:
1. Set the temperature of Grill to 450 degrees F and preheat with closed lid for 15 minutes.
2. In a metal pan, add all ingredients except for lobster tails and mix well.
3. Place the pan onto the grill and cook for about 10 minutes.
4. Meanwhile, cut down the top of the shell and expose lobster meat.
5. Remove pan of butter mixture from grill.
6. Coat the lobster meat with butter mixture.
7. Place the lobster tails onto the grill and cook for about 15 minutes, coating with butter mixture once halfway through.
8. Remove from grill and serve hot.

Nutrition Info: Calories per serving: 409; Carbohydrates: 0.6g; Protein: 43.5g; Fat: 24.9g; Sugar: 0.1g; Sodium: 1305mg; Fiber: 0g

5.   Blackened Catfish

Servings: 4
Cooking Time: 40 Minutes
Ingredients:
- Spice blend
- 1teaspoon granulated garlic
- 1/4 teaspoon cayenne pepper
- 1/2 cup Cajun seasoning
- 1teaspoon ground thyme
- 1teaspoon ground oregano
- 1teaspoon onion powder
- 1tablespoon smoked paprika
- 1teaspoon pepper
- Fish
- 4 catfish fillets
- Salt to taste
- 1/2 cup butter

Directions:
1. In a bowl, combine all the ingredients for the spice blend.
2. Sprinkle both sides of the fish with the salt and spice blend.
3. Set your wood pellet grill to 450 degrees F.
4. Heat your cast iron pan and add the butter. Add the fillets to the pan.
5. Cook for 5 minutes per side.
6. Serving Suggestion: Garnish with lemon wedges.
7. Tip: Smoke the catfish for 20 minutes before seasoning.

Nutrition Info: Calories: 181.5 Fat: 10.5 g Cholesterol: 65.8 mg Carbohydrates: 2.9 g Fiber: 1.8 g Sugars: 0.4 g Protein: 19.2 g

6.   Grilled Rainbow Trout

Servings: 6
Cooking Time: 2 Hours
Ingredients:
- 6 rainbow trout, cleaned, butterfly
- For the Brine:
- 1/4 cup salt
- 1 tablespoon ground black pepper
- 1/2 cup brown sugar
- 2 tablespoons soy sauce
- 16 cups water

Directions:
1. Prepare the brine and for this, take a large container, add all of its ingredients in it, stir until sugar has dissolved, then add trout and let soak for 1 hour in the refrigerator.
2. When ready to cook, switch on the grill, fill the grill hopper with oak flavored wood pellets, power the grill on by using the control panel, select 'smoke' on the temperature dial, or set the temperature to 225 degrees F and let it preheat for a minimum of 15 minutes.
3. Meanwhile, remove trout from the brine and pat dry with paper towels.
4. When the grill has preheated, open the lid, place trout on the grill grate, shut the grill and smoke for 2 hours until thoroughly cooked and tender.
5. When done, transfer trout to a dish and then serve.

Nutrition Info: Calories: 250 Cal ;Fat: 12 g ;Carbs: 1.4 g ;Protein: 33 g ;Fiber: 0.3 g

7.   Grilled Lingcod

Servings: 6
Cooking Time: 15 Minutes
Ingredients:
- 2 lb lingcod fillets
- 1/2 tbsp salt
- 1/2 tbsp white pepper
- 1/4 tbsp cayenne
- Lemon wedges

Directions:
1. Preheat the wood pellet grill to 375°F.
2. Place the lingcod on a parchment paper and season it with salt, white pepper, cayenne pepper then top with the lemon.
3. Place the fish on the grill and cook for 15 minutes or until the internal temperature reaches 145°F.
4. Serve and enjoy.

Nutrition Info: Calories 245, Total fat 2g, Saturated fat 0g, Total Carbs 2g, Net Carbs 1g, Protein 52g, Sugar 1g, Fiber 1g, Sodium: 442mg, Potassium 649mg

8.   Salmon With Avocado Salsa

Servings: 6
Cooking Time: 20 Minutes
Ingredients:
- 3 lb. salmon fillet
- Garlic salt and pepper to taste
- 4 cups avocado, sliced into cubes
- 1 onion, chopped
- 1 jalapeño pepper, minced
- 1 tablespoon lime juice
- 1 tablespoon olive oil
- ¼ cup cilantro, chopped
- Salt to taste

Directions:
1. Sprinkle both sides of salmon with garlic salt and pepper.
2. Set the wood pellet grill to smoke.
3. Grill the salmon for 7 to 8 minutes per side.
4. While waiting, prepare the salsa by combining the remaining ingredients in a bowl.
5. Serve salmon with the avocado salsa.
6. Tips: You can also use tomato salsa for this recipe if you don't have avocados.

9.   Wood Pellet Grilled Scallops

Servings: 4
Cooking Time: 15 Minutes
Ingredients:
- 2 lb sea scallops, dried with a paper towel
- 1/2 tbsp garlic salt
- 2 tbsp kosher salt
- 4 tbsp salted butter
- Squeeze lemon juice

Directions:
1. Preheat the wood pellet grill to 400°F with the cast pan inside.
2. Sprinkle with both salts, pepper on both sides of the scallops.
3. Place the butter on the cast iron then add the scallops. Close the lid and cook for 8 minutes.
4. Flip the scallops and close the lid once more. Cook for 8 more minutes.
5. Remove the scallops from the grill and give a lemon squeeze. Serve immediately and enjoy.

Nutrition Info: Calories 177, Total fat 7g, Saturated fat 4g, Total Carbs 6g, Net Carbs 6g, Protein 23g, Sugar 0g, Fiber 0g, Sodium: 1430mg, Potassium 359mg

10.   Fish Fillets With Pesto

Servings: 6
Cooking Time: 15 Minutes
Ingredients:
- 2 cups fresh basil
- 1 cup parsley, chopped
- 1/2 cup walnuts
- 1/2 cup olive oil
- 1 cup Parmesan cheese, grated
- Salt and pepper to taste
- 4 white fish fillets

Directions:
1. Preheat the wood pellet grill to high for 15 minutes while the lid is closed.
2. Add all the ingredients except fish to a food processor.
3. Pulse until smooth. Set aside.
4. Season fish with salt and pepper.
5. Grill for 6 to 7 minutes per side.
6. Serve with the pesto sauce.
7. Tips: You can also spread a little bit of the pesto on the fish before grilling.

11.   Summer Paella

Servings: 6
Cooking Time: 45 Minutes
Ingredients:
- 6 tablespoons extra-virgin olive oil, divided, plus more for drizzling
- 2 green or red bell peppers, cored, seeded, and diced
- 2 medium onions, diced
- 2 garlic cloves, slivered
- 1 (29-ounce) can tomato purée
- 1½ pounds chicken thighs
- Kosher salt
- 1½ pounds tail-on shrimp, peeled and deveined
- 1 cup dried thinly sliced chorizo sausage
- 1 tablespoon smoked paprika
- 1½ teaspoons saffron threads
- 2 quarts chicken broth
- 3½ cups white rice
- 2 (7½-ounce) cans chipotle chiles in adobo sauce
- 1½ pounds fresh clams, soaked in cold water for 15 to 20 minutes2 tablespoons chopped fresh parsley
- 2 lemons, cut into wedges, for serving

Directions:
1. Make the sofrito: On the stove top, in a saucepan over medium-low heat, combine ¼ cup of olive oil, the bell peppers, onions, and garlic, and cook for 5 minutes, or until the onions are translucent.
2. Stir in the tomato purée, reduce the heat to low, and simmer, stirring frequently, until most of the liquid has evaporated, about 30 minutes. Set aside. (Note: The sofrito can be made in advance and refrigerated.)
3. Supply your smoker with wood pellets and follow the manufacturer's specific start-up procedure. Preheat, with the lid closed, to 450°F.
4. Heat a large paella pan on the smoker and add the remaining 2 tablespoons of olive oil.
5. Add the chicken thighs, season lightly with salt, and brown for 6 to 10 minutes, then push to the outer edge of the pan.
6. Add the shrimp, season with salt, close the lid, and smoke for 3 minutes.
7. Add the sofrito, chorizo, paprika, and saffron, and stir together.
8. In a separate bowl, combine the chicken broth, uncooked rice, and 1 tablespoon of salt, stirring until well combined.
9. Add the broth-rice mixture to the paella pan, spreading it evenly over the other ingredients.
10. Close the lid and smoke for 5 minutes, then add the chipotle chiles and clams on top of the rice.
11. Close the lid and continue to smoke the paella for about 30 minutes, or until all of the liquid is absorbed.
12. Remove the pan from the grill, cover tightly with aluminum foil, and let rest off the heat for 5 minutes.
13. Drizzle with olive oil, sprinkle with the fresh parsley, and serve with the lemon wedges.

12.   Grilled Tuna

Servings: 4
Cooking Time: 4 Minutes
Ingredients:
- 4 (6 ounce each) tuna steaks (1 inch thick)
- 1 lemon (juiced)
- 1 clove garlic (minced)
- 1 tsp chili
- 2 tbsp extra virgin olive oil
- 1 cup white wine
- 3 tbsp brown sugar
- 1 tsp rosemary

Directions:
1. Combine lemon, chili, white wine, sugar, rosemary, olive oil and garlic. Add the tuna steaks and toss to combine.
2. Transfer the tuna and marinade to a zip-lock bag. Refrigerate for 3 hours.
3. Remove the tuna steaks from the marinade and let them rest for about 1 hour
4. Start your grill on smoke, leaving the lid opened for 5 minutes, or until fire starts.
5. Do not open lid to preheat until 15 minutes to the setting "HIGH"
6. Grease the grill grate with oil and place the tuna on the grill grate. Grill tuna steaks for 4 minutes, 2 minutes per side.
7. Remove the tuna from the grill and let them rest for a few minutes.
Nutrition Info: Calories: 137 Cal Fat: 17.8 g Carbohydrates: 10.2 g   Protein: 51.2 g Fiber: 0.6 g

13.   Citrus-smoked Trout

Servings: 6
Cooking Time: 1 To 2 Hours
Ingredients:
- 6 to 8 skin-on rainbow trout, cleaned and scaled
- 1 gallon orange juice
- ½ cup packed light brown sugar
- ¼ cup salt
- 1 tablespoon freshly ground black pepper
- Nonstick spray, oil, or butter, for greasing
- 1 tablespoon chopped fresh parsley
- 1 lemon, sliced

Directions:
1. Fillet the fish and pat dry with paper towels.
2. Pour the orange juice into a large container with a lid and stir in the brown sugar, salt, and pepper.
3. Place the trout in the brine, cover, and refrigerate for 1 hour.
4. Cover the grill grate with heavy-duty aluminum foil. Poke holes in the foil and spray with cooking spray (see Tip).
5. Supply your smoker with wood pellets and follow the manufacturer's specific start-up procedure. Preheat, with the lid closed, to 225°F.
6. Remove the trout from the brine and pat dry. Arrange the fish on the foil-covered grill grate, close the lid, and smoke for 1 hour 30 minutes to 2 hours, or until flaky.
7. Remove the fish from the heat. Serve garnished with the fresh parsley and lemon slices.

14. Grilled Lingcod

Servings: 6
Cooking Time: 15 Minutes
Ingredients:
- 2 lb lingcod fillets
- 1/2 tbsp salt
- 1/2 tbsp white pepper
- 1/4 tbsp cayenne pepper
- Lemon wedges

Directions:
1. Preheat your to 375F.
2. Place the lingcod on a parchment paper or on a grill mat
3. Season the fish with salt, pepper, and top with lemon wedges.
4. Cook the fish for 15 minutes or until the internal temperature reaches 145F.

Nutrition Info: Calories 245, Total fat 2g, Saturated fat 0g, Total carbs 2g, Net carbs 0g Protein 52g, Sugars 1g, Fiber 1g, Sodium 442mg

15. Wood Pellet Grilled Lobster Tail

Servings: 2
Cooking Time: 15 Minutes
Ingredients:
- 10 oz lobster tail
- 1/4 tbsp old bay seasoning
- 1/4 tbsp Himalayan sea salt
- 2 tbsp butter, melted
- 1 tbsp fresh parsley, chopped

Directions:
1. Preheat the wood pellet to 450°F.
2. Slice the tails down the middle using a knife.
3. Season with seasoning and salt then place the tails on the grill grate.
4. Grill for 15 minutes or until the internal temperature reaches 140°F..
5. Remove the tails and drizzle with butter and garnish with parsley.
6. Serve and enjoy.

Nutrition Info: Calories 305, Total fat 14g, Saturated fat 8g, Total Carbs 5g, Net Carbs 5g, Protein 18g, Sugar 0g, Fiber 0g, Sodium: 685mg, Potassium 159mg

16. Barbecued Shrimp

Servings: 4
Cooking Time: 10 Minutes
Ingredients:
- 1 pound peeled and deveined shrimp, with tails on
- 2 tablespoons olive oil
- 1 batch Dill Seafood Rub

Directions:
1. Soak wooden skewers in water for 30 minutes.
2. Supply your smoker with wood pellets and follow the manufacturer's specific start-up procedure. Preheat the grill, with the lid closed, to 375°F.
3. Thread 4 or 5 shrimp per skewer.
4. Coat the shrimp all over with olive oil and season each side of the skewers with the rub.
5. Place the skewers directly on the grill grate and grill the shrimp for 5 minutes per side. Remove the skewers from the grill and serve immediately.

17. Spicy Shrimp

Servings: 4
Cooking Time: 10 Minutes

Ingredients:
- 3 tablespoons olive oil
- 6 cloves garlic
- 2 tablespoons chicken dry rub
- 6 oz. chili
- 1 1/2 tablespoons white vinegar
- 1 1/2 teaspoons sugar
- 2 lb. shrimp, peeled and deveined

Directions:
1. Add olive oil, garlic, dry rub, chili, vinegar and sugar in a food processor.
2. Blend until smooth.
3. Transfer mixture to a bowl.
4. Stir in shrimp.
5. Cover and refrigerate for 30 minutes.
6. Preheat the wood pellet grill to hit for 15 minutes while the lid is closed.
7. Thread shrimp onto skewers.
8. Grill for 3 minute per side.
9. Tips: You can also add vegetables to the skewers.

18. Lively Flavored Shrimp

Servings: 6
Cooking Time: 30 Minutes

Ingredients:
- 8 oz. salted butter, melted
- ¼ C. Worcestershire sauce
- ¼ C. fresh parsley, chopped
- 1 lemon, quartered
- 2 lb. jumbo shrimp, peeled and deveined
- 3 tbsp. BBQ rub

Directions:
1. In a metal baking pan, add all ingredients except for shrimp and BBQ rub and mix well.
2. Season the shrimp with BBQ rub evenly.
3. Add the shrimp in the pan with butter mixture and coat well.
4. Set aside for about 20-30 minutes.
5. Set the temperature of Grill to 250 degrees F and preheat with closed lid for 15 minutes.
6. Place the pan onto the grill and cook for about 25-30 minutes.
7. Remove the pan from grill and serve hot.

Nutrition Info: Calories per serving: 462; Carbohydrates: 4.7g; Protein: 34.9g; Fat: 33.3g; Sugar: 2.1g; Sodium: 485mg; Fiber: 0.2g

19.   Cajun Smoked Catfish

Servings: 4
Cooking Time: 2 Hours
Ingredients:

- 4 catfish fillets (5 ounces each)
- ½ cup Cajun seasoning
- 1 tsp ground black pepper
- 1 tbsp smoked paprika
- 1 /4 tsp cayenne pepper
- 1 tsp hot sauce
- 1 tsp granulated garlic
- 1 tsp onion powder
- 1 tsp thyme
- 1 tsp salt or more to taste
- 2 tbsp chopped fresh parsley

Directions:
1.   Pour water into the bottom of a square or rectangular dish. Add 4 tbsp salt. Arrange the catfish fillets into the dish. Cover the dish and refrigerate for 3 to 4 hours.
2.   Combine the paprika, cayenne, hot sauce, onion, salt, thyme, garlic, pepper and Cajun seasoning in a mixing bowl.
3.   Remove the fish from the dish and let it sit for a few minutes, or until it is at room temperature. Pat the fish fillets dry with a paper towel.
4.   Rub the seasoning mixture over each fillet generously.
5.   Start your grill on smoke, leaving the lid opened for 5 minutes, or until fire starts.
6.   Keep lid unopened and preheat to 200°F, using mesquite hardwood pellets.
7.   Arrange the fish fillets onto the grill grate and close the grill. Cook for about 2 hours, or until the fish is flaky.
8.   Remove the fillets from the grill and let the fillets rest for a few minutes to cool.
9.   Serve and garnish with chopped fresh parsley.
Nutrition Info: Calories: 204 Cal Fat: 11.1 g Carbohydrates: 2.7 g   Protein: 22.9 g Fiber: 0.6 g

20.   Dijon-smoked Halibut

Servings: 6
Cooking Time: 2 Hours
Ingredients:

- 4 (6-ounce) halibut steaks
- ¼ cup extra-virgin olive oil
- 2 teaspoons kosher salt
- 1 teaspoon freshly ground black pepper
- ½ cup mayonnaise
- ½ cup sweet pickle relish
- ¼ cup finely chopped sweet onion
- ¼ cup chopped roasted red pepper
- ¼ cup finely chopped tomato
- ¼ cup finely chopped cucumber
- 2 tablespoons Dijon mustard
- 1 teaspoon minced garlic

Directions:
1.   Rub the halibut steaks with the olive oil and season on both sides with the salt and pepper. Transfer to a plate, cover with plastic wrap, and refrigerate for 4 hours.
2.   Supply your smoker with wood pellets and follow the manufacturer's specific start-up procedure. Preheat, with the lid closed, to 200°F.
3.   Remove the halibut from the refrigerator and rub with the mayonnaise.
4.   Put the fish directly on the grill grate, close the lid, and smoke for 2 hours, or until opaque and an instant-read thermometer inserted in the fish reads 140°F.
5.   While the fish is smoking, combine the pickle relish, onion, roasted red pepper, tomato, cucumber, Dijon mustard, and garlic in a medium bowl. Refrigerate the mustard relish until ready to serve.
6.   Serve the halibut steaks hot with the mustard relish.

21.   Oysters In The Shell

Servings: 4
Cooking Time: 20 Minutes
Ingredients:
- 8 medium oysters, unopened, in the shell, rinsed and scrubbed
- 1 batch Lemon Butter Mop for Seafood

Directions:
1.   Supply your smoker with wood pellets and follow the manufacturer's specific start-up procedure. Preheat the grill, with the lid closed, to 375°F.
2.   Place the unopened oysters directly on the grill grate and grill for about 20 minutes, or until the oysters are done and their shells open.
3.   Discard any oysters that do not open. Shuck the remaining oysters, transfer them to a bowl, and add the mop. Serve immediately.

22.   Cider Salmon

Servings: 4
Cooking Time: 1 Hour
Ingredients:
- 1 ½ pound salmon fillet, skin-on, center-cut, pin bone removed
- For the Brine:
- 4 juniper berries, crushed
- 1 bay leaf, crumbled
- 1 piece star anise, broken
- 1 1/2 cups apple cider
- For the Cure:
- 1/2 cup salt
- 1 teaspoon ground black pepper
- 1/4 cup brown sugar
- 2 teaspoons barbecue rub

Directions:
1.   Prepare the brine and for this, take a large container, add all of its ingredients in it, stir until mixed, then add salmon and let soak for a minimum of 8 hours in the refrigerator.
2.   Meanwhile, prepare the cure and for this, take a small bowl, place all of its ingredients in it and stir until combined.
3.   After 8 hours, remove salmon from the brine, then take a baking dish, place half of the cure in it, top with salmon skin-side down, sprinkle remaining cure on top, cover with plastic wrap and let it rest for 1 hour in the refrigerator.
4.   When ready to cook, switch on the grill, fill the grill hopper with oak flavored wood pellets, power the grill on by using the control panel, select 'smoke' on the temperature dial, or set the temperature to 200 degrees F and let it preheat for a minimum of 5 minutes.
5.   Meanwhile, remove salmon from the cure, pat dry with paper towels, and then sprinkle with black pepper.
6.   When the grill has preheated, open the lid, place salmon on the grill grate, shut the grill, and smoke for 1 hour until the internal temperature reaches 150 degrees F.
7.   When done, transfer salmon to a cutting board, let it rest for 5 minutes, then remove the skin and serve.
Nutrition Info: Calories: 233 Cal ;Fat: 14 g ;Carbs: 0 g ;Protein: 25 g ;Fiber: 0 g

23.   Wood Pellet Smoked Buffalo Shrimp

Servings: 6
Cooking Time: 5 Minutes
Ingredients:
- 1 lb raw shrimps peeled and deveined
- 1/2 tbsp salt
- 1/4 tbsp garlic salt
- 1/4 tbsp garlic powder
- 1/4 tbsp onion powder
- 1/2 cup buffalo sauce

Directions:
1. Preheat the wood pellet grill to 450°F.
2. Coat the shrimp with both salts, garlic and onion powders.
3. Place the shrimp in a grill and cook for 3 minutes on each side.
4. Remove from the grill and toss in buffalo sauce. Serve with cheese, celery and napkins. Enjoy.

Nutrition Info: Calories 57, Total fat 1g, Saturated fat 0g, Total Carbs 1g, Net Carbs 1g, Protein 10g, Sugar 0g, Fiber 0g, Sodium: 1106mg, Potassium 469mg.

24.   Halibut With Garlic Pesto

Servings: 4
Cooking Time: 10 Minutes
Ingredients:
- 4 halibut fillets
- 1 cup olive oil
- Salt and pepper to taste
- 1/4 cup garlic, chopped
- 1/4 cup pine nuts

Directions:
1. Set the wood pellet grill to smoke.
2. Establish fire for 5 minutes.
3. Set temperature to high.
4. Place a cast iron on a grill.
5. Season fish with salt and pepper.
6. Add fish to the pan.
7. Drizzle with a little oil.
8. Sear for 4 minutes per side.
9. Prepare the garlic pesto by pulsing the remaining ingredients in the food processor until smooth.
10. Serve fish with garlic pesto.
11. Tips: You can also use other white fish fillets for this recipe.

25.   Wood Pellet Teriyaki Smoked Shrimp

Servings: 6
Cooking Time: 10 Minutes
Ingredients:
- 1 lb tail-on shrimp, uncooked
- 1/2 tbsp onion powder
- 1/2 tbsp salt
- 1/2 tbsp Garlic powder
- 4 tbsp Teriyaki sauce
- 4 tbsp sriracha mayo
- 2 tbsp green onion, minced

Directions:
1. Peel the shrimps leaving the tails then wash them removing any vein left over. Drain and pat with a paper towel to drain.
2. Preheat the wood pellet to 450°F
3. Season the shrimp with onion, salt, and garlic then place it on the grill to cook for 5 minutes on each side.
4. Remove the shrimp from the grill and toss it with teriyaki sauce. Serve garnished with mayo and onions. Enjoy.

Nutrition Info: Calories 87, Total fat 0g, Saturated fat 0g, Total Carbs 2g, Net Carbs 2g, Protein 16g, Sugar 1g, Fiber 0g, Sodium: 1241mg

26.   Omega-3 Rich Salmon

Servings: 6
Cooking Time: 20 Minutes
Ingredients:
- 6 (6-oz.) skinless salmon fillets
- 1/3 C. olive oil
- ¼ C. spice rub
- ¼ C. honey
- 2 tbsp. Sriracha
- 2 tbsp. fresh lime juice

Directions:
1. Set the temperature of Grill to 300 degrees F and preheat with closed lid for 15 minutes.
2. Coat salmon fillets with olive oil and season with rub evenly.
3. In a small bowl, mix together remaining ingredients.
4. Arrange salmon fillets onto the grill, flat-side up and cook for about 7-10 minutes per side, coating with honey mixture once halfway through.
5. Serve hot alongside remaining honey mixture.

Nutrition Info: Calories per serving: 384; Carbohydrates: 15.7g; Protein: 33g; Fat: 21.7g; Sugar: 11.6g; Sodium: 621mg; Fiber: 0g

27.   Blackened Salmon

Servings: 4
Cooking Time: 30 Minutes
Ingredients:
- 2 lb. salmon, fillet, scaled and deboned
- 2 tablespoons olive oil
- 4 tablespoons sweet dry rub
- 1 tablespoon cayenne pepper
- 2 cloves garlic, minced

Directions:
1. Turn on your wood pellet grill.
2. Set it to 350 degrees F.
3. Brush the salmon with the olive oil.
4. Sprinkle it with the dry rub, cayenne pepper, and garlic.
5. Grill for 5 minutes per side.

Nutrition Info: Calories: 460Fat: 23 gCholesterol: 140 mgCarbohydrates: 7 g Fiber: 5 g Sugars: 2 g Protein: 50 g

28.   Bacon-wrapped Shrimp

Servings: 12
Cooking Time: 10 Minutes
Ingredients:
- 1 lb raw shrimp
- 1/2 tbsp salt
- 1/4 tbsp garlic powder
- 1 lb bacon, cut into halves

Directions:
1. Preheat your to 350F.
2. Remove the shells and tails from the shrimp then pat them dry with the paper towels.
3. Sprinkle salt and garlic on the shrimp then wrap with bacon and secure with a toothpick.
4. Place the shrimps on a baking rack greased with cooking spray.
5. Cook for 10 minutes, flip and cook for another 10 minutes or until the bacon is crisp enough.
6. Remove from the and serve.

Nutrition Info: Calories 204, Total fat 14g, Saturated fat 5g, Total carbs 1g, Net carbs 1g Protein 18g, Sugars 0g, Fiber 0g, Sodium 939mg

29.   Seared Tuna Steaks

Servings: 2
Cooking Time: 10 Minutes
Ingredients:
- 2 (1½- to 2-inch-thick) tuna steaks
- 2 tablespoons olive oil
- Salt
- Freshly ground black pepper

Directions:
1.   Supply your smoker with wood pellets and follow the manufacturer's specific start-up procedure. Preheat the grill, with the lid closed, to 500°F.
2.   Rub the tuna steaks all over with olive oil and season both sides with salt and pepper.
3.   Place the tuna steaks directly on the grill grate and grill for 3 to 5 minutes per side, leaving a pink center. Remove the tuna steaks from the grill and serve immediately.

30.   Peppercorn Tuna Steaks

Servings: 3
Cooking Time: 10 Minutes
Ingredients:
- ¼ cup of salt
- 2 pounds yellowfin tuna
- ¼ cup Dijon mustard
- Freshly ground black pepper
- 2 tablespoons peppercorn

Directions:
1.   Take a large-sized container and dissolve salt in warm water (enough water to cover fish)
2.   Transfer tuna to the brine and cover, refrigerate for 8 hours
3.   Preheat your smoker to 250 degrees Fahrenheit with your preferred wood
4.   Remove tuna from bring and pat it dry
5.   Transfer to grill pan and spread Dijon mustard all over
6.   Season with pepper and sprinkle peppercorn on top
7.   Transfer tuna to smoker and smoker for 1 hour
8.   Enjoy!
Nutrition Info: Calories: 707 Fats: 57g Carbs: 10g Fiber: 2g

31.   Grilled Herbed Tuna

Servings: 6
Cooking Time: 10 Minutes
Ingredients:
- 6 tuna steaks
- 1 tablespoon lemon zest
- 1 tablespoon fresh thyme, chopped
- 1 tablespoon fresh parsley, chopped
- Garlic salt to taste

Directions:
1.   Sprinkle the tuna steaks with lemon zest, herbs and garlic salt.
2.   Cover with foil.
3.   Refrigerate for 4 hours.
4.   Grill for 3 minutes per side.
5.   Tips: Take the fish out of the refrigerator 30 minutes before cooking.

32.   Grilled Shrimp Kabobs

Servings: 4
Cooking Time: 10 Minutes
Ingredients:
- 1 lb. colossal shrimp, peeled and deveined
- 2 tbsp. oil
- 1/2 tbsp. garlic salt
- 1/2 tbsp. salt
- 1/8 tbsp. pepper
- 6 skewers

Directions:
1. Preheat your to 375F.
2. Pat the shrimp dry with a paper towel.
3. In a mixing bowl, mix oil, garlic salt, salt, and pepper
4. Toss the shrimp in the mixture until well coated.
5. Skewer the shrimps and cook in the with the lid closed for 4 minutes.
6. Open the lid, flip the skewers and cook for another 4 minutes or until the shrimp is pink and the flesh is opaque.
7. Serve.

Nutrition Info: Calories 325, Total fat 0g, Saturated fat 0g, Total carbs 0g, Net carbs 0g Protein 20g, Sugars 0g, Fiber 0g, Sodium 120mg

33.   Mussels With Pancetta Aïoli

Servings: 4
Cooking Time: 30 Minutes
Ingredients:
- ¾ cup mayonnaise (to make your own, see page 460)
- 1tablespoon minced garlic, or more to taste
- 1.4-ounce slice pancetta, chopped
- Salt and pepper
- 4 pounds mussels
- 8 thick slices Italian bread
- ¼ cup good-quality olive oil

Directions:
1. Whisk the mayonnaise and garlic together in a small bowl. Put the pancetta in a small cold skillet, turn the heat to low; cook, occasionally stir, until most of the fat is rendered and the meat turns golden and crisp about 5 minutes. Drain on a paper towel, then stir into the mayonnaise along with 1 teaspoon of the rendered fat from the pan. Taste and add more garlic and some salt if you like. Cover and refrigerate until you're ready to serve. (You can make the aïoli up to several days ahead; refrigerate in an airtight container.)
2. Start the coals or heat a gas grill for direct hot cooking. Make sure the grates are clean.
3. Rinse the mussels and pull off any beards. Discard any that are broken or don't close when tapped.
4. Brush both sides of the bread slices with the oil. Put the bread on the grill directly over the fire. Close the lid and toast, turning once, until it develops grill marks with some charring, 1 to 2 minutes per side. Remove from the grill and keep warm.
5. Scatter the mussels onto the grill directly over the fire, spreading them out, so they are in a single layer. Immediately close the lid and cook for 3 minutes. Transfer the open mussels to a large bowl with tongs. If any have not opened, leave them on the grill, close the lid, and cook for another minute or 2, checking frequently and removing open mussels until they are all off the grill.
6. Dollop the aïoli over the tops of the mussels and use a large spoon to turn them over to coat them. Serve the mussels drizzled with their juices, either over (or alongside) the bread.

Nutrition Info: Calories: 159 Fats: 6.1 g Cholesterol: 0 mg Carbohydrates: 14.95 g Fiber: 0 g Sugars: 0 g Proteins: 9.57 g

34.   Lobster Tails

Servings: 4
Cooking Time: 35 Minutes
Ingredients:
- 2 lobster tails, each about 10 ounces
- For the Sauce:
- 2 tablespoons chopped parsley
- 1/4 teaspoon garlic salt
- 1 teaspoon paprika
- 1/4 teaspoon ground black pepper
- 1/4 teaspoon old bay seasoning
- 8 tablespoons butter, unsalted
- 2 tablespoons lemon juice

Directions:
1. Switch on the grill, fill the grill hopper with flavored wood pellets, power the grill on by using the control panel, select 'smoke' on the temperature dial, or set the temperature to 450 degrees F and let it preheat for a minimum of 15 minutes.
2. Meanwhile, prepare the sauce and for this, take a small saucepan, place it over medium-low heat, add butter in it and when it melts, add remaining ingredients for the sauce and stir until combined, set aside until required.
3. Prepare the lobster and for this, cut the shell from the middle to the tail by using kitchen shears and then take the meat from the shell, keeping it attached at the base of the crab tail.
4. Then butterfly the crab meat by making a slit down the middle, then place lobster tails on a baking sheet and pour 1 tablespoon of sauce over each lobster tail, reserve the remaining sauce.
5. When the grill has preheated, open the lid, place crab tails on the grill grate, shut the grill and smoke for 30 minutes until opaque.
6. When done, transfer lobster tails to a dish and then serve with the remaining sauce.

Nutrition Info: Calories: 290 Cal ;Fat: 22 g ;Carbs: 1 g ;Protein: 20 g ;Fiber: 0.3 g

35.   Spot Prawn Skewers

Servings: 6
Cooking Time: 10 Minutes
Ingredients:
- 2 lb spot prawns
- 2 tbsp oil
- Salt and pepper to taste

Directions:
1. Preheat your to 400F.
2. Skewer your prawns with soaked skewers then generously sprinkle with oil, salt, and pepper.
3. Place the skewers on the grill and cook with the lid closed for 5 minutes on each side.
4. Remove the skewers and serve when hot.

Nutrition Info: Calories 221, Total fat 7g, Saturated fat 1g, Total carbs 2g, Net carbs 2g Protein 34g, Sugars 0g, Fiber 0g, Sodium 1481mg

36.   Yummy Buttery Clams

Servings: 6
Cooking Time: 8 Minutes
Ingredients:
- 24 littleneck clams
- ½ C. cold butter, chopped
- 2 tbsp. fresh parsley, minced
- 3 garlic cloves, minced
- 1 tsp. fresh lemon juice

Directions:
1.   Set the temperature of Grill to 450 degrees F and preheat with closed lid for 15 minutes.
2.   Scrub the clams under cold running water.
3.   In a large casserole dish, mix together remaining ingredients.
4.   Place the casserole dish onto the grill.
5.   Now, arrange the clams directly onto the grill and cook for about 5-8 minutes or until they are opened. (Discard any that fail to open).
6.   With tongs, carefully transfer the opened clams into the casserole dish and remove from grill.
7.   Serve immediately.

Nutrition Info: Calories per serving: 306; Carbohydrates: 6.4g; Protein: 29.3g; Fat: 7.6g; Sugar: 0.1g; Sodium: 237mg; Fiber: 0.1g

37.   Smoked Scallops

Servings: 6
Cooking Time: 15 Minutes
Ingredients:
- 2 pounds sea scallops
- 4 tbsp salted butter
- 2 tbsp lemon juice
- ½ tsp ground black pepper
- 1 garlic clove (minced)
- 1 kosher tsp salt
- 1 tsp freshly chopped tarragon

Directions:
1.   Let the scallops dry using paper towels and drizzle all sides with salt and pepper to season
2.   Place you're a cast iron pan in your grill and preheat the grill to 400°F with lid closed for 15 minutes.
3.   Combine the butter and garlic in hot cast iron pan. Add the scallops and stir. Close grill lid and cook for 8 minutes. Flip the scallops and cook for an additional 7 minutes.
4.   Remove the scallop from heat and let it rest for a few minutes.
5.   Stir in the chopped tarragon. Serve and top with lemon juice.

Nutrition Info: Calories: 204 Cal Fat: 8.9 g Carbohydrates: 4 g   Protein: 25.6 g Fiber: 0.1 g

38.   Cod With Lemon Herb Butter

Servings: 4
Cooking Time: 15 Minutes
Ingredients:
- 4 tablespoons butter
- 1 clove garlic, minced
- 1 tablespoon tarragon, chopped
- 1 tablespoon lemon juice
- 1 teaspoon lemon zest
- Salt and pepper to taste
- 1 lb. cod fillet

Directions:
1. Preheat the wood pellet grill to high for 15 minutes while the lid is closed.
2. In a bowl, mix the butter, garlic, tarragon, lemon juice and lemon zest, salt and pepper.
3. Place the fish in a baking pan.
4. Spread the butter mixture on top.
5. Bake the fish for 15 minutes.
6. Tips: You can also use other white fish fillet for this recipe.

39.   Mango Shrimp

Servings: 4
Cooking Time: 15 Minutes
Ingredients:
- 1lb. shrimp, peeled and deveined but tail intact
- 2tablespoons olive oil
- Mango seasoning

Directions:
1. Turn on your wood pellet grill.
2. Preheat it to 425 degrees F.
3. Coat the shrimp with the oil and season with the mango seasoning.
4. Thread the shrimp into skewers.
5. Grill for 3 minutes per side.
6. Serving Suggestion: Garnish with chopped parsley.

Nutrition Info: Calories: 223.1 Fat: 4.3 g Cholesterol: 129.2 mg Carbohydrates: 29.2 g Fiber: 4.4 g Sugars: 15. 6g Protein: 19.5 g

40.   Wood-fired Halibut

Servings: 4
Cooking Time: 20 Minutes
Ingredients:
- 1 pound halibut fillet
- 1 batch Dill Seafood Rub

Directions:
1. Supply your smoker with wood pellets and follow the manufacturer's specific start-up procedure. Preheat the grill, with the lid closed, to 325°F.
2. Sprinkle the halibut fillet on all sides with the rub. Using your hands, work the rub into the meat.
3. Place the halibut directly on the grill grate and grill until its internal temperature reaches 145°F. Remove the halibut from the grill and serve immediately.

41.   Rockfish

Servings: 6
Cooking Time: 20 Minutes
Ingredients:
- 6 rockfish fillets
- 1 lemon, sliced
- 3/4 tbsp salt
- 2 tbsp fresh dill, chopped
- 1/2 tbsp garlic powder
- 1/2 tbsp onion powder
- 6 tbsp butter

Directions:
1. Preheat your to 400F.
2. Season the fish with salt, dill, garlic and onion powder on both sides then place it in a baking dish.
3. Place a pat of butter and a lemon slice on each fillet. Place the baking dish in the and close the lid.
4. Cook for 20 minutes or until the fish is no longer translucent and is flaky.
5. Remove from and let rest for 5 minutes before serving.

Nutrition Info: Calories 270, Total fat 17g, Saturated fat 9g, Total carbs 2g, Net carbs 2g Protein 28g, Sugars 0g, Fiber 0g, Sodium 381mg

42.   Charleston Crab Cakes With Remoulade

Servings: 4
Cooking Time: 45 Minutes
Ingredients:

- 1¼ cups mayonnaise
- ¼ cup yellow mustard
- 2 tablespoons sweet pickle relish, with its juices
- 1 tablespoon smoked paprika
- 2 teaspoons Cajun seasoning
- 2 teaspoons prepared horseradish
- 1 teaspoon hot sauce
- 1 garlic clove, finely minced
- 2 pounds fresh lump crabmeat, picked clean
- 20 butter crackers (such as Ritz brand), crushed
- 2 tablespoons Dijon mustard
- 1 cup mayonnaise
- 2 tablespoons freshly squeezed lemon juice
- 1 tablespoon salted butter, melted
- 1 tablespoon Worcestershire sauce
- 1 tablespoon Old Bay seasoning
- 2 teaspoons chopped fresh parsley
- 1 teaspoon ground mustard
- 2 eggs, beaten
- ¼ cup extra-virgin olive oil, divided

Directions:

1. For the remoulade:
2. In a small bowl, combine the mayonnaise, mustard, pickle relish, paprika, Cajun seasoning, horseradish, hot sauce, and garlic.
3. Refrigerate until ready to serve.
4. For the crab cakes:
5. Supply your smoker with wood pellets and follow the manufacturer's specific start-up procedure. Preheat, with the lid closed, to 375°F.
6. Spread the crabmeat on a foil-lined baking sheet and place over indirect heat on the grill, with the lid closed, for 30 minutes.
7. Remove from the heat and let cool for 15 minutes.
8. While the crab cools, combine the crushed crackers, Dijon mustard, mayonnaise, lemon juice, melted butter, Worcestershire sauce, Old Bay, parsley, ground mustard, and eggs until well incorporated.
9. Fold in the smoked crabmeat, then shape the mixture into 8 (1-inch-thick) crab cakes.
10. In a large skillet or cast-iron pan on the grill, heat 2 tablespoons of olive oil. Add half of the crab cakes, close the lid, and smoke for 4 to 5 minutes on each side, or until crispy and golden brown.
11. Remove the crab cakes from the pan and transfer to a wire rack to drain. Pat them to remove any excess oil.
12. Repeat steps 6 and 7 with the remaining oil and crab cakes.
13. Serve the crab cakes with the remoulade.

43.   Pacific Northwest Salmon

Servings: 4
Cooking Time: 1 Hour, 15 Minutes
Ingredients:
- 1 (2-pound) half salmon fillet
- 1 batch Dill Seafood Rub
- 2 tablespoons butter, cut into 3 or 4 slices

Directions:
1.   Supply your smoker with wood pellets and follow the manufacturer's specific start-up procedure. Preheat the grill, with the lid closed, to 180°F.
2.   Season the salmon all over with the rub. Using your hands, work the rub into the flesh.
3.   Place the salmon directly on the grill grate, skin-side down, and smoke for 1 hour.
4.   Place the butter slices on the salmon, equally spaced. Increase the grill's temperature to 300°F and continue to cook until the salmon's internal temperature reaches 145°F. Remove the salmon from the grill and serve immediately.

44.   Wood Pellet Smoked Salmon

Servings: 8
Cooking Time: 4 Hours
Ingredients:
- Brine
- 4 cups water
- 1 cup brown sugar
- 1/3 cup kosher salt
- Salmon
- Salmon fillet, skin in
- Maple syrup

Directions:
1.   Combine all the brine ingredients until the sugar has fully dissolved.
2.   Add the brine to a ziplock bag with the salmon and refrigerate for 12 hours.
3.   Remove the salmon from the brine, wash it and rinse with water. Pat dry with paper towel then let sit at room temperature for 2 hours.
4.   Startup your wood pellet to smoke and place the salmon on a baking rack sprayed with cooking spray.
5.   After cooking for an hour, baste the salmon with maple syrup. Do not let the smoker get above 180°F for accurate results.
6.   Smoke for 3-4 hours or until the salmon flakes easily.
Nutrition Info: Calories 101, Total fat 2g, Saturated fat 0g, Total carbs 16g, Net carbs 16g, Protein 4g, Sugar 16g, Fiber 0g, Sodium: 3131mg

45.   Wood Pellet Salt And Pepper Spot Prawn Skewers

Servings: 6
Cooking Time: 10 Minutes
Ingredients:
- 2 lb spot prawns, clean
- 2 tbsp oil
- Salt and pepper to taste

Directions:
1.   Preheat your grill to 400°F.
2.   Meanwhile, soak the skewers then skewer with the prawns.
3.   Brush with oil then season with salt and pepper to taste.
4.   Place the skewers in the grill, close the lid, and cook for 5 minutes on each side.
5.   Remove from the grill and serve. Enjoy.
Nutrition Info: Calories 221, Total fat 7g, Saturated fat 1g, Total Carbs 2g, Net Carbs 2g, Protein 34g, Sugar 0g, Fiber 0g, Sodium: 1481mg, Potassium 239mg

46.   Smoked Shrimp

Servings: 4
Cooking Time: 10 Minutes
Ingredients:
- 4 tablespoons olive oil
- 1 tablespoon Cajun seasoning
- 2 cloves garlic, minced
- 1 tablespoon lemon juice
- Salt to taste
- 2 lb. shrimp, peeled and deveined

Directions:
1. Combine all the ingredients in a sealable plastic bag.
2. Toss to coat evenly.
3. Marinate in the refrigerator for 4 hours.
4. Set the wood pellet grill to high.
5. Preheat it for 15 minutes while the lid is closed.
6. Thread shrimp onto skewers.
7. Grill for 4 minutes per side.
8. Tips: Soak skewers first in water if you are using wooden skewers.

47.   Super-tasty Trout

Servings: 8
Cooking Time: 5 Hours
Ingredients:
- 1 (7-lb.) whole lake trout, butterflied
- ½ C. kosher salt
- ½ C. fresh rosemary, chopped
- 2 tsp. lemon zest, grated finely

Directions:
1. Rub the trout with salt generously and then, sprinkle with rosemary and lemon zest.
2. Arrange the trout in a large baking dish and refrigerate for about 7-8 hours.
3. Remove the trout from baking dish and rinse under cold running water to remove the salt.
4. With paper towels, pat dry the trout completely.
5. Arrange a wire rack in a sheet pan.
6. Place the trout onto the wire rack, skin side down and refrigerate for about 24 hours.
7. Set the temperature of Grill to 180 degrees F and preheat with closed lid for 15 minutes, using charcoal.
8. Place the trout onto the grill and cook for about 2-4 hours or until desired doneness.
9. Remove the trout from grill and place onto a cutting board for about 5 minutes before serving.

Nutrition Info: Calories per serving: 633; Carbohydrates: 2.4g; Protein: 85.2g; Fat: 31.8g; Sugar: 0g; Sodium: 5000mg; Fiber: 1.6g

48.   No-fuss Tuna Burgers

Servings: 6
Cooking Time: 15 Minutes
Ingredients:
- 2 lb. tuna steak
- 1 green bell pepper, seeded and chopped
- 1 white onion, chopped
- 2 eggs
- 1 tsp. soy sauce
- 1 tbsp. blackened Saskatchewan rub
- Salt and freshly ground black pepper, to taste

Directions:
1. Set the temperature of Grill to 500 degrees F and preheat with closed lid for 15 minutes.
2. In a bowl, add all the ingredients and mix until well combined.
3. With greased hands, make patties from mixture.
4. Place the patties onto the grill close to the edges and cook for about 10-15 minutes, flipping once halfway through.
5. Serve hot.

Nutrition Info: Calories per serving: 313; Carbohydrates: 3.4g; Protein: 47.5g; Fat: 11g; Sugar: 1.9g; Sodium: 174mg; Fiber: 0.7g

49.   Wood Pellet Rockfish

Servings: 6
Cooking Time: 20 Minutes
Ingredients:
- 6 rockfish fillets
- 1 lemon, sliced
- 3/4 tbsp Himalayan salt
- 2 tbsp fresh dill, chopped
- 1/2 tbsp garlic powder
- 1/2 tbsp onion powder
- 6 tbsp butter

Directions:
1. Preheat your wood pellet grill to 375°F.
2. Place the rockfish in a baking dish and season with salt, dill, garlic, and onion.
3. Place butter on top of the fish then close the lid. Cook for 20 minutes or until the fish is no longer translucent.
4. Remove from grill and let sit for 5 minutes before serving. enjoy.

Nutrition Info: Calories 270, Total fat 17g, Saturated fat 9g, Total Carbs 2g, Net Carbs 0g, Protein 28g, Sugar 0g, Fiber 0g, Sodium: 381mg

50.   Halibut

Servings: 4
Cooking Time: 30 Minutes
Ingredients:
- 1-pound fresh halibut filet (cut into 4 equal sizes)
- 1 tbsp fresh lemon juice
- 2 garlic cloves (minced)
- 2 tsp soy sauce
- ½ tsp ground black pepper
- ½ tsp onion powder
- 2 tbsp honey
- ½ tsp oregano
- 1 tsp dried basil
- 2 tbsp butter (melted)
- Maple syrup for serving

Directions:
1. Combine the lemon juice, honey, soy sauce, onion powder, oregano, dried basil, pepper and garlic.
2. Brush the halibut filets generously with the filet the mixture. Wrap the filets with aluminum foil and refrigerate for 4 hours.
3. Remove the filets from the refrigerator and let them sit for about 2 hours, or until they are at room temperature.
4. Activate your wood pellet grill on smoke, leaving the lid opened for 5 minutes or until fire starts.
5. The lid must not be opened for it to be preheated and reach 275°F 15 minutes, using fruit wood pellets.
6. Place the halibut filets directly on the grill grate and smoke for 30 minutes
7. Remove the filets from the grill and let them rest for 10 minutes.
8. Serve and top with maple syrup to taste

Nutrition Info: Calories: 180 Cal Fat: 6.3 g Carbohydrates: 10 g   Protein: 20.6 g Fiber: 0.3 g

51. Buttered Crab Legs

Servings: 4
Cooking Time: 10 Minutes
Ingredients:
- 12 tablespoons butter
- 1 tablespoon parsley, chopped
- 1 tablespoon tarragon, chopped
- 1 tablespoon chives, chopped
- 1 tablespoon lemon juice
- 4 lb. king crab legs, split in the center

Directions:
1. Set the wood pellet grill to 375 degrees F.
2. Preheat it for 15 minutes while lid is closed.
3. In a pan over medium heat, simmer the butter, herbs and lemon juice for 2 minutes.
4. Place the crab legs on the grill.
5. Pour half of the sauce on top.
6. Grill for 10 minutes.
7. Serve with the reserved butter sauce.
8. Tips: You can also use shrimp for this recipe.

52. Juicy Smoked Salmon

Servings: 5
Cooking Time: 50 Minutes
Ingredients:
- ½ cup of sugar
- 2 tablespoon salt
- 2 tablespoons crushed red pepper flakes
- ½ cup fresh mint leaves, chopped
- ¼ cup brandy
- 1(4 pounds) salmon, bones removed
- 2cups alder wood pellets, soaked in water

Directions:
1. Take a medium-sized bowl and add brown sugar, crushed red pepper flakes, mint leaves, salt, and brandy until a paste forms
2. Rub the paste all over your salmon and wrap the salmon with a plastic wrap
3. Allow them to chill overnight
4. Preheat your smoker to 220 degrees Fahrenheit and add wood Pellets
5. Transfer the salmon to the smoker rack and cook smoke for 45 minutes
6. Once the salmon has turned red-brown and the flesh flakes off easily, take it out and serve!

Nutrition Info: Calories: 370 Fats: 28g Carbs: 1g Fiber: 0g

Servings: 6
Cooking Time: 30 Minutes
Ingredients:
- Lemon cream sauce
- 4 garlic cloves
- 1 shallot
- 1 leek
- 2 tbsp olive oil
- 1 tbsp salt
- 1/4 tbsp black pepper
- 3 tbsp butter
- 1/4 cup white wine
- 1 cup whipping cream
- 2 tbsp lemon juice
- 1 tbsp lemon zest
- Crab mix
- 1 lb crab meat
- 1/3 cup mayo
- 1/3 cup sour cream
- 1/3 cup lemon cream sauce
- 1/4 green onion, chopped
- 1/4 tbsp black pepper
- 1/2 tbsp old bay seasoning
- Fish
- 2 lb lingcod
- 1 tbsp olive oil
- 1 tbsp salt
- 1 tbsp paprika
- 1 tbsp green onion, chopped
- 1 tbsp Italian parsley

Directions:
1. Lemon cream sauce
2. Chop garlic, shallot, and leeks then add to a saucepan with oil, salt, pepper, and butter.
3. Saute over medium heat until the shallot is translucent.
4. Deglaze with white wine then add whipping cream. Bring the sauce to boil, reduce heat and simmer for 3 minutes.
5. Remove from heat and add lemon juice and lemon zest. Transfer the sauce to a blender and blend until smooth.
6. Set aside 1/3 cup for the crab mix
7. Crab mix
8. Add all the ingredients in a mixing bowl and mix thoroughly until well combined.
9. Set aside
10. Fish
11. Fire up your to high heat then slice the fish into 6-ounce portions.
12. Lay the fish on its side on a cutting board and slice it 3/4 way through the middle leaving a 1/2 inch on each end so as to have a nice pouch.
13. Rub the oil into the fish then place them on a baking sheet. Sprinkle with salt.
14. Stuff crab mix into each fish then sprinkle paprika and place it on the grill.
15. Cook for 15 minutes or more if the fillets are more than 2 inches thick.
16. Remove the fish and transfer to serving platters. Pour the remaining lemon cream sauce on each fish and garnish with onions and parsley.

Nutrition Info: Calories 476, Total fat 33g, Saturated fat 14g, Total carbs 6g, Net carbs 5g Protein 38g, Sugars 3g, Fiber 1g, Sodium 1032mg

54.   Jerk Shrimp

Servings: 12
Cooking Time: 6 Minutes
Ingredients:
- 2 pounds shrimp, peeled, deveined
- 3 tablespoons olive oil
- For the Spice Mix:
- 1 teaspoon garlic powder
- 1 teaspoon of sea salt
- 1/4 teaspoon ground cayenne
- 1 tablespoon brown sugar
- 1/8 teaspoon smoked paprika
- 1 tablespoon smoked paprika
- 1/4 teaspoon ground thyme
- 1 lime, zested

Directions:
1.   Switch on the grill, fill the grill hopper with flavored wood pellets, power the grill on by using the control panel, select 'smoke' on the temperature dial, or set the temperature to 450 degrees F and let it preheat for a minimum of 5 minutes.
2.   Meanwhile, prepare the spice mix and for this, take a small bowl, place all of its ingredients in it and stir until mixed.
3.   Take a large bowl, place shrimps in it, sprinkle with prepared spice mix, drizzle with oil and toss until well coated.
4.   When the grill has preheated, open the lid, place shrimps on the grill grate, shut the grill and smoke for 3 minutes per side until firm and thoroughly cooked.
5.   When done, transfer shrimps to a dish and then serve.
Nutrition Info: Calories: 131 Cal ;Fat: 4.3 g ;Carbs: 0 g ;Protein: 22 g ;Fiber: 0 g

55.   Wood Pellet Grilled Salmon Sandwich

Servings: 4
Cooking Time: 15 Minutes
Ingredients:
- Salmon Sandwiches
- 4 salmon fillets
- 1 tbsp olive oil
- Fin and feather rub
- 1 tbsp salt
- 4 toasted bun
- Butter lettuce
- Dill Aioli
- 1/2 cup mayonnaise
- 1/2 tbsp lemon zest
- 2 tbsp lemon juice
- 1/4 tbsp salt
- 1/2 tbsp fresh dill, minced

Directions:
1.   Mix all the dill aioli ingredients and place them in the fridge.
2.   Preheat the wood pellet grill to 450°F.
3.   Brush the salmon fillets with oil, rub, and salt. Place the fillets on the grill and cook until the internal temperature reaches 135°F.
4.   Remove the fillets from the grill and let rest for 5 minutes.
5.   Spread the aioli on the buns then top with salmon, lettuce, and the top bun.
6.   Serve when hot.
Nutrition Info: Calories 852, Total fat 54g, Saturated fat 10g, Total Carbs 30g, Net Carbs 28g, Protein 57g, Sugar 5g, Fiber 2g, Sodium: 1268mg, Potassium 379mg

56.   Grilled Shrimp

Servings: 4
Cooking Time: 15 Minutes
Ingredients:
- Jumbo shrimp peeled and cleaned - 1 lb.
- Oil - 2 tbsp
- Salt - ½ tbsp
- Skewers - 4-5
- Pepper - ⅛ tbsp
- Garlic salt - ½ tbsp

Directions:
1. Preheat the wood pellet grill to 375 degrees.
2. Mix all the ingredients in a small bowl.
3. After washing and drying the shrimp, mix it well with the oil and seasonings.
4. Add skewers to the shrimp and set the bowl of shrimp aside.
5. Open the skewers and flip them.
6. Cook for 4 more minutes. Remove when the shrimp is opaque and pink.

Nutrition Info: Carbohydrates: 1.3 g Protein: 19 g Fat: 1.4 g Sodium: 805 mg Cholesterol: 179 mg

57.   Grilled Tilapia

Servings: 6
Cooking Time: 20 Minutes
Ingredients:
- 2 tsp dried parsley
- ½ tsp garlic powder
- 1 tsp cayenne pepper
- ½ tsp ground black pepper
- ½ tsp thyme
- ½ tsp dried basil
- ½ tsp oregano
- 3 tbsp olive oil
- ½ tsp lemon pepper
- 1 tsp kosher salt
- 1 lemon (juiced)
- 6 tilapia fillets
- 1 ½ tsp creole seafood seasoning

Directions:
1. In a mixing bowl, combine spices
2. Brush the fillets with oil and lemon juice.
3. Liberally, season all sides of the tilapia fillets with the seasoning mix.
4. Preheat your grill to 325°F
5. Place a non-stick BBQ grilling try on the grill and arrange the tilapia fillets onto it.
6. Grill for 15 to 20 minutes
7. Remove fillets and cool down

Nutrition Info: Calories: 176 Cal Fat: 9.6 g Carbohydrates: 1.5 g   Protein: 22.3 g Fiber: 0.5 g

58.   Cajun Seasoned Shrimp

Servings: 4
Cooking Time: 16-20 Minutes
Ingredients:
- 20 pieces of jumbo Shrimp
- 1/2 teaspoon of Cajun seasoning
- 1tablespoon of Canola oil
- 1teaspoon of magic shrimp seasoning

Directions:
1. Take a large bowl and add canola oil, shrimp, and seasonings.
2. Mix well for fine coating.
3. Now put the shrimp on skewers.
4. Put the grill grate inside the grill and set a timer to 8 minutes at high for preheating.
5. Once the grill is preheated, open the unit and place the shrimp skewers inside.
6. Cook the shrimp for 2 minutes.
7. Open the unit to flip the shrimp and cook for another 2 minutes at medium.
8. Own done, serve.

Nutrition Info: Calories: 382 Total Fat: 7.4g Saturated Fat: 0g Cholesterol: 350mg Sodium: 2208mg Total Carbohydrate: 23.9g Dietary Fiber 2.6g Total Sugars: 2.6g Protein: 50.2g

59.   Citrus Salmon

Servings: 6
Cooking Time: 30 Minutes
Ingredients:
- 2 (1-lb.) salmon fillets
- Salt and freshly ground black pepper, to taste
- 1 tbsp. seafood seasoning
- 2 lemons, sliced
- 2 limes, sliced

Directions:
1. Set the temperature of Grill to 225 degrees F and preheat with closed lid for 15 minutes.
2. Season the salmon fillets with salt, black pepper and seafood seasoning evenly.
3. Place the salmon fillets onto the grill and top each with lemon and lime slices evenly.
4. Cook for about 30 minutes.
5. Remove the salmon fillets from grill and serve hot.

Nutrition Info: Calories per serving: 327; Carbohydrates: 1g; Protein: 36.1g; Fat: 19.8g; Sugar: 0.2g; Sodium: 237mg; Fiber: 0.3g

60.   Bbq Oysters

Servings: 4-6
Cooking Time: 16 Minutes
Ingredients:
- Shucked oysters - 12
- Unsalted butter - 1 lb.
- Chopped green onions - 1 bunch
- Honey Hog BBQ Rub or Meat Church "The Gospel" - 1 tbsp
- Minced green onions - ½ bunch
- Seasoned breadcrumbs - ½ cup
- Cloves of minced garlic - 2
- Shredded pepper jack cheese - 8 oz
- Heat and Sweet BBQ sauce

Directions:
1. Preheat the pellet grill for about 10-15 minutes with the lid closed.
2. To make the compound butter, wait for the butter to soften. Then combine the butter, onions, BBQ rub, and garlic thoroughly.
3. Lay the butter evenly on plastic wrap or parchment paper. Roll it up in a log shape and tie the ends with butcher's twine. Place these in the freezer to solidify for an hour. This butter can be used on any kind of grilled meat to enhance its flavor. Any other high-quality butter can also replace this compound butter.
4. Shuck the oysters, keeping the juice in the shell.
5. Sprinkle all the oysters with breadcrumbs and place them directly on the grill. Allow them to cook for 5 minutes. You will know they are cooked when the oysters begin to curl slightly at the edges.
6. Once they are cooked, put a spoonful of the compound butter on the oysters. Once the butter melts, you can add a little bit of pepper jack cheese to add more flavor to them.
7. The oysters must not be on the grill for longer than 6 minutes, or you risk overcooking them. Put a generous squirt of the BBQ sauce on all the oysters. Also, add a few chopped onions.
8. Allow them to cool for a few minutes and enjoy the taste of the sea!
Nutrition Info: Carbohydrates: 2.5 g Protein: 4.7 g Fat: 1.1 g Sodium: 53 mg Cholesterol: 25 mg

61.   Oyster In Shells

Servings: 4
Cooking Time: 8 Minutes
Ingredients:
- 12 medium oysters
- 1 tsp oregano
- 1 lemon (juiced)
- 1 tsp freshly ground black pepper
- 6 tbsp unsalted butter (melted)
- 1 tsp salt or more to taste
- 2 garlic cloves (minced)
- 2 ½ tbsp grated parmesan cheese
- 2 tbsp freshly chopped parsley

Directions:
1. Remove dirt
2. Open the shell completely. Discard the top shell.
3. Gently run the knife under the oyster to loosen the oyster foot from the bottom shell.
4. Repeat step 2 and 3 for the remaining oysters.
5. Combine melted butter, lemon, pepper, salt, garlic and oregano in a mixing bowl.
6. Pour ½ to 1 tsp of the butter mixture on each oyster.
7. Start your wood pellet grill on smoke, leaving the lid opened for 5 minutes, or until fire starts.
8. Keep lid unopened to preheat in the set "HIGH" with lid closed for 15 minutes.
9. Gently arrange the oysters onto the grill grate.
10. Grill oyster for 6 to 8 minutes or until the oyster juice is bubbling and the oyster is plump.
11. Remove oysters from heat. Serve and top with grated parmesan and chopped parsley.
Nutrition Info: Calories: 200 Cal Fat: 19.2 g Carbohydrates: 3.9 g   Protein: 4.6 g Fiber: 0.8 g

62.   Lobster Tail

Servings: 2
Cooking Time: 15 Minutes
Ingredients:
- 10 oz lobster tail
- 1/4 tbsp old bay seasoning
- 1/4 tbsp Himalayan salt
- 2 tbsp butter, melted
- 1 tbsp fresh parsley, chopped

Directions:
1. Preheat your to 450F.
2. Slice the tail down the middle then season it with bay seasoning and salt.
3. Place the tails directly on the grill with the meat side down. Grill for 15 minutes or until the internal temperature reaches 140F.
4. Remove from the and drizzle with butter.
5. Serve when hot garnished with parsley.

Nutrition Info: Calories 305, Total fat 14g, Saturated fat 8g, Total carbs 5g, Net carbs 5g Protein 38g, Sugars 0g, Fiber 0g, Sodium 684mg

63.   Barbeque Shrimp

Servings: 6
Cooking Time: 8 Minutes
Ingredients:
- 2-pound raw shrimp (peeled and deveined)
- ¼ cup extra virgin olive oil
- ½ tsp paprika
- ½ tsp red pepper flakes
- 2 garlic cloves (minced)
- 1 tsp cumin
- 1 lemon (juiced)
- 1 tsp kosher salt
- 1 tbsp chili paste
- Bamboo or wooden skewers (soaked for 30 minutes, at least)

Directions:
1. Combine the pepper flakes, cumin, lemon, salt, chili, paprika, garlic and olive oil. Add the shrimp and toss to combine.
2. Transfer the shrimp and marinade into a zip-lock bag and refrigerate for 4 hours.
3. Let shrimp rest in room temperature after pulling it out from marinade
4. Start your grill on smoke, leaving the lid opened for 5 minutes, or until fire starts. Use hickory wood pellet.
5. Keep lid unopened and preheat the grill to "high" for 15 minutes.
6. Thread shrimps onto skewers and arrange the skewers on the grill grate.
7. Smoke shrimps for 8 minutes, 4 minutes per side.
8. Serve and enjoy.

Nutrition Info: Calories: 267 Cal Fat: 11.6 g Carbohydrates: 4.9 g   Protein: 34.9 g Fiber:0.4 g

64.   Cured Cold-smoked Lox

Servings: 6
Cooking Time: 6 Hours
Ingredients:
- ¼ cup salt
- ¼ cup sugar
- 1 tablespoon freshly ground black pepper
- 1 bunch dill, chopped
- 1 pound sashimi-grade salmon, skin removed
- 1 avocado, sliced
- 8 bagels
- 4 ounces cream cheese
- 1 bunch alfalfa sprouts
- 1 (5-ounce) jar capers

Directions:
1.   In a small bowl, combine the salt, sugar, pepper, and fresh dill to make the curing mixture. Set aside.
2.   On a smooth surface, lay out a large piece of plastic wrap and spread half of the curing salt mixture in the middle, spreading it out to about the size of the salmon.
3.   Place the salmon on top of the curing salt.
4.   Top the fish with the remaining curing salt, covering it completely. Wrap the salmon, leaving the ends open to drain.
5.   Place the wrapped fish in a rimmed baking pan or dish lined with paper towels to soak up liquid.
6.   Place a weight on the salmon evenly, such as a pan with a couple of heavy jars of pickles on top.
7.   Put the salmon pan with weights in the refrigerator. Place something (a dishtowel, for example) under the back of the pan in order to slightly tip it down so the liquid drains away from the fish.
8.   Leave the salmon to cure in the refrigerator for 24 hours.
9.   Place the wood pellets in the smoker, but do not follow the start-up procedure and do not preheat.
10.   Remove the salmon from the refrigerator, unwrap it, rinse it off, and pat dry.
11.   Put the salmon in the smoker while still cold from the refrigerator to slow down the cooking process. You'll need to use a cold-smoker attachment or enlist the help of a smoker tube to hold the temperature at 80°F and maintain that for 6 hours to absorb smoke and complete the cold-smoking process.
12.   Remove the salmon from the smoker, place it in a sealed plastic bag, and refrigerate for 24 hours. The salmon will be translucent all the way through.
13.   Thinly slice the lox and serve with sliced avocado, bagels, cream cheese, alfalfa sprouts, and capers.

65.   Sriracha Salmon

Servings: 4
Cooking Time: 25 Minutes
Ingredients:
- 3-pound salmon, skin on
- For the Marinade:
- 1 teaspoon lime zest
- 1 tablespoon minced garlic
- 1 tablespoon grated ginger
- Sea salt as needed
- Ground black pepper as needed
- 1/4 cup maple syrup
- 2 tablespoons soy sauce
- 2 tablespoons Sriracha sauce
- 1 tablespoon toasted sesame oil
- 1 tablespoon rice vinegar
- 1 teaspoon toasted sesame seeds

Directions:
1.   Prepare the marinade and for this, take a small bowl, place all of its ingredients in it, stir until well combined, and then pour the mixture into a large plastic bag.
2.   Add salmon in the bag, seal it, turn it upside down to coat salmon with the marinade and let it marinate for a minimum of 2 hours in the refrigerator.
3.   When ready to cook, switch on the grill, fill the grill hopper with flavored wood pellets, power the grill on by using the control panel, select 'smoke' on the temperature dial, or set the temperature to 450 degrees F and let it preheat for a minimum of 5 minutes.
4.   Meanwhile, take a large baking sheet, line it with parchment paper, place salmon on it skin-side down and then brush with the marinade.
5.   When the grill has preheated, open the lid, place baking sheet containing salmon on the grill grate, shut the grill and smoke for 25 minutes until thoroughly cooked.
6.   When done, transfer salmon to a dish and then serve.
Nutrition Info: Calories: 360 Cal ;Fat: 21 g ;Carbs: 28 g ;Protein: 16 g ;Fiber: 1.5 g

POULTRY RECIPES

66.   Grilled Buffalo Chicken

Servings: 6
Cooking Time: 20 Minutes
Ingredients:
- 5 chicken breasts, boneless and skinless
- 2 tbsp homemade BBQ rub
- 1 cup homemade Cholula Buffalo sauce

Directions:
1.   Preheat the to 400F.
2.   Slice the chicken breast lengthwise into strips. Season the slices with BBQ rub.
3.   Place the chicken slices on the grill and paint both sides with buffalo sauce.
4.   Cook for 4 minutes with the lid closed. Flip the breasts, paint again with sauce and cook until the internal temperature reaches 165F.
5.   Remove the chicken from the and serve when warm.
Nutrition Info: Calories 176, Total fat 4g, Saturated fat 1g, Total carbs 1g, Net carbs 1g Protein 32g, Sugars 1g, Fiber 0g, Sodium 631mg

67.   Wood Pellet Grilled Buffalo Chicken Leg

Servings: 6
Cooking Time: 25 Minutes
Ingredients:
- 12 chicken legs
- 1/2 tbsp salt
- 1 tbsp buffalo seasoning
- 1 cup buffalo sauce

Directions:
1.   Preheat your wood pellet grill to 325°F.
2.   Toss the legs in salt and buffalo seasoning then place them on the preheated grill.
3.   Grill for 40 minutes ensuring you turn them twice through the cooking.
4.   Brush the legs with buffalo sauce and cook for an additional 10 minutes or until the internal temperature reaches 165°F.
5.   Remove the legs from the grill, brush with more sauce, and serve when hot.
Nutrition Info: Calories: 956 Cal Fat: 47 g Carbohydrates: 1 g   Protein: 124 g Fiber: 0 g

68.   Cornish Game Hen

Servings: 4
Cooking Time: 2 To 3 Hours
Ingredients:
- 4 Cornish game hens
- Extra-virgin olive oil, for rubbing
- 2 teaspoons salt
- 1 teaspoon freshly ground black pepper
- 1 teaspoon celery seeds

Directions:
1.   Supply your smoker with wood pellets and follow the manufacturer's specific start-up procedure. Preheat, with the lid closed, to 275°F.
2.   Rub the game hens over and under the skin with olive oil and season all over with the salt, pepper, and celery seeds.
3.   Place the birds directly on the grill grate, close the lid, and smoke for 2 to 3 hours, or until a meat thermometer inserted in each bird reads 170°F.
4.   Serve the Cornish game hens hot.

69.   Rustic Maple Smoked Chicken Wings

Servings: 16
Cooking Time: 35 Minutes
Ingredients:
- 16 chicken wings
- 1 tablespoon olive oil
- 1 tablespoon Chicken Rub
- 1 cup 'Que BBQ Sauce or other commercial BBQ sauce of choice

Directions:
1. Place all ingredients in a bowl except for the BBQ sauce. Massage the chicken breasts so that it is coated with the marinade.
2. Place in the fridge to marinate for at least 4 hours.
3. Fire the Grill to 350F. Use maple wood pellets. Close the grill lid and preheat for 15 minutes.
4. Place the wings on the grill grate and cook for 12 minutes on each side with the lid closed.
5. Once the chicken wings are done, place in a clean bowl.
6. Pour over the BBQ sauce and toss to coat with the sauce.

Nutrition Info: Calories per serving: 230 ; Protein: 37.5g; Carbs: 2.2g; Fat: 7g Sugar: 1.3g

70.   Wood Pellet Smoked Cornish Hens

Servings: 6
Cooking Time: 1 Hour
Ingredients:
- 6 Cornish hens
- 3 tbsp avocado oil
- 6 tbsp rub of choice

Directions:
1. Fire up the wood pellet and preheat it to 275°F.
2. Rub the hens with oil then coat generously with rub. Place the hens on the grill with the chest breast side down.
3. Smoke for 30 minutes. Flip the hens and increase the grill temperature to 400°F. Cook until the internal temperature reaches 165°F.
4. Remove from the grill and let rest for 10 minutes before serving. Enjoy.

Nutrition Info: Calories: 696 Cal Fat: 50 g Carbohydrates: 1 g   Protein: 57 g Fiber: 0 g

71.   Wood Pellet Smoked Spatchcock Turkey

Servings: 6
Cooking Time: 1 Hour 45 Minutes
Ingredients:
- 1 whole turkey
- 1/2 cup oil
- 1/4 cup chicken rub
- 1 tbsp onion powder
- 1 tbsp garlic powder
- 1 tbsp rubbed sage

Directions:
1. Preheat your wood pellet grill to high.
2. Meanwhile, place the turkey on a platter with the breast side down then cut on either side of the backbone to remove the spine.
3. Flip the turkey and season on both sides then place it on the preheated grill or on a pan if you want to catch the drippings.
4. Grill on high for 30 minutes, reduce the temperature to 325°F, and grill for 45 more minutes or until the internal temperature reaches 165°F
5. Remove from the grill and let rest for 20 minutes before slicing and serving. Enjoy.

Nutrition Info: Calories 156, Total fat 16g, Saturated fat 2g, Total Carbs 1g, Net Carbs 1g, Protein 2g, Sugar 0g, Fiber 0g, Sodium: 19mg

72.   Smoked Lemon Chicken Breasts

Servings: 6
Cooking Time: 30 Minutes
Ingredients:
- 2 lemons, zested and juiced
- 1 clove of garlic, minced
- 2 teaspoons honey
- 2 teaspoons salt
- 1 teaspoon ground black pepper
- 2 sprigs fresh thyme
- ½ cup olive oil
- 6 boneless chicken breasts

Directions:
1. Place all ingredients in a bowl. Massage the chicken breasts so that it is coated with the marinade.
2. Place in the fridge to marinate for at least 4 hours.
3. Fire the Grill to 350F. Use apple wood pellets. Close the grill lid and preheat for 15 minutes.
4. Place the chicken breasts on the grill grate and cook for 15 minutes on both sides.
5. Serve immediately or drizzle with lemon juice.

Nutrition Info: Calories per serving: 671 ; Protein: 60.6 g; Carbs: 3.5 g; Fat: 44.9g Sugar: 2.3g

73.   Lemon Rosemary And Beer Marinated Chicken

Servings: 6
Cooking Time: 55 Minutes
Ingredients:
- 1 whole chicken
- 1 lemon, zested and juiced
- 1 teaspoon salt
- 1 teaspoon ground black pepper
- 1 teaspoon rosemary, chopped
- 12-ounce beer, apple-flavored

Directions:
1. Place all ingredients in a bowl and allow the chicken to marinate for at least 12 hours in the fridge.
2. When ready to cook, fire the Grill to 350F. Use preferred wood pellets. Close the grill lid and preheat for 15 minutes.
3. Place the chicken on the grill grate and cook for 55 minutes.
4. Cook until the internal temperature reads at 165F.
5. Take the chicken out and allow to rest before carving.

Nutrition Info: Calories per serving: 288; Protein: 36.1g; Carbs: 4.4g; Fat: 13.1g Sugar: 0.7g

Servings: 4-6
Cooking Time: 40 Minutes

Ingredients:

- Corn - ½ cup
- Leftover wild turkey meat - 2 cups
- Black beans - ½ cup
- Taco seasoning - 3 tbsp
- Water ½ cup
- Rotel chilies and tomatoes - 1 can
- Egg roll wrappers- 12
- Cloves of minced garlic- 4
- 1 chopped Poblano pepper or 2 jalapeno peppers
- Chopped white onion - ½ cup

Directions:

1. Add some olive oil to a fairly large skillet. Heat it over medium heat on a stove.
2. Add peppers and onions. Sauté the mixture for 2-3 minutes until it turns soft.
3. Add some garlic and sauté for another 30 seconds. Add the Rotel chilies and beans to the mixture. Keeping mixing the content gently. Reduce the heat and then simmer.
4. After about 4-5 minutes, pour in the taco seasoning and ⅓ cup of water over the meat. Mix everything and coat the meat thoroughly. If you feel that it is a bit dry, you can add 2 tbsp of water. Keep cooking until everything is heated all the way through.
5. Remove the content from the heat and box it to store in a refrigerator. Before you stuff the mixture into the egg wrappers, it should be completely cool to avoid breaking the rolls.
6. Place a spoonful of the cooked mixture in each wrapper and then wrap it securely and tightly. Do the same with all the wrappers.
7. Preheat the pellet grill and brush it with some oil. Cook the egg rolls for 15 minutes on both sides until the exterior is nice and crispy.
8. Remove them from the grill and enjoy with your favorite salsa!

Nutrition Info: Carbohydrates: 26.1 g Protein: 9.2 g Fat: 4.2 g Sodium: 373.4 mg Cholesterol: 19.8 mg

75.   Teriyaki Wings

Servings: 8
Cooking Time: 50 Minutes
Ingredients:
- 2 ½ pounds large chicken wings
- 1 tablespoon toasted sesame seeds
- For the Marinade:
- 2 scallions, sliced
- 2 tablespoons grated ginger
- ½ teaspoon minced garlic
- 1/4 cup brown sugar
- 1/2 cup soy sauce
- 2 tablespoon rice wine vinegar
- 2 teaspoons sesame oil
- 1/4 cup water

Directions:
1.   Prepare the chicken wings and for this, remove tips from the wings, cut each chicken wing through the joint into three pieces, and then place in a large plastic bag.
2.   Prepare the sauce and for this, take a small saucepan, place it over medium-high heat, add all of its ingredients in it, stir until mixed, and bring it to a boil.
3.   Then switch heat to medium level, simmer the sauce for 10 minutes, and when done, cool the sauce completely.
4.   Pour the sauce over chicken wings, seal the bag, turn it upside down to coat chicken wings with the sauce and let it marinate for a minimum of 8 hours in the refrigerator.
5.   When ready to cook, switch on the grill, fill the grill hopper with maple-flavored wood pellets, power the grill on by using the control panel, select 'smoke' on the temperature dial, or set the temperature to 350 degrees F and let it preheat for a minimum of 15 minutes.
6.   Meanwhile,
7.   When the grill has preheated, open the lid, place chicken wings on the grill grate, shut the grill and smoke for 50 minutes until crispy and meat is no longer pink, turning halfway.
8.   When done, transfer chicken wings to a dish, sprinkle with sesame seeds and then serve.
Nutrition Info: Calories: 150 Cal ;Fat: 7.5 g ;Carbs: 6 g ;Protein: 12 g ;Fiber: 1 g

76.   Sweet Sriracha Bbq Chicken

Servings: 5
Cooking Time: 1 And ½-2 Hours
Ingredients:
- 1cup sriracha
- ½ cup butter
- ½ cup molasses
- ½ cup ketchup
- ¼ cup firmly packed brown sugar
- 1teaspoon salt
- 1teaspoon fresh ground black pepper
- 1whole chicken, cut into pieces
- ½ teaspoon fresh parsley leaves, chopped

Directions:
1.   Preheat your smoker to 250 degrees Fahrenheit using cherry wood
2.   Take a medium saucepan and place it over low heat, stir in butter, sriracha, ketchup, molasses, brown sugar, mustard, pepper and salt and keep stirring until the sugar and salt dissolves
3.   Divide the sauce into two portions
4.   Brush the chicken half with the sauce and reserve the remaining for serving
5.   Make sure to keep the sauce for serving on the side, and keep the other portion for basting
6.   Transfer chicken to your smoker rack and smoke for about 1 and a ½ to 2 hours until the internal temperature reaches 165 degrees Fahrenheit
7.   Sprinkle chicken with parsley and serve with reserved BBQ sauce
8.   Enjoy!
Nutrition Info: Calories: 148 Fats: 0.6g Carbs: 10g Fiber: 1g

77. Chili Barbecue Chicken

Servings: 4
Cooking Time: 2 Hours And 10 Minutes
Ingredients:
- 1 tablespoon brown sugar
- 1 tablespoon lime zest
- 1 tablespoon chili powder
- 1/2 teaspoon ground cumin
- 1/2 tablespoon ground espresso
- Salt to taste
- 2 tablespoons olive oil
- 8 chicken legs
- 1/2 cup barbecue sauce

Directions:
1. Combine sugar, lime zest, chili powder, cumin, ground espresso and salt.
2. Drizzle the chicken legs with oil.
3. Sprinkle sugar mixture all over the chicken.
4. Cover with foil and refrigerate for 5 hours.
5. Set the wood pellet grill to 180 degrees F.
6. Preheat it for 15 minutes while the lid is closed.
7. Smoke the chicken legs for 1 hour.
8. Increase temperature to 350 degrees F.
9. Grill the chicken legs for another 1 hour, flipping once.
10. Brush the chicken with barbecue sauce and grill for another 10 minutes.
11. Tips: You can also add chili powder to the barbecue sauce.

78. Crispy & Juicy Chicken

Servings: 6
Cooking Time: 5 Hours
Ingredients:
- ¾ C. dark brown sugar
- ½ C. ground espresso beans
- 1 tbsp. ground cumin
- 1 tbsp. ground cinnamon
- 1 tbsp. garlic powder
- 1 tbsp. cayenne pepper
- Salt and freshly ground black pepper, to taste
- 1 (4-lb.) whole chicken, neck and giblets removed

Directions:
1. Set the temperature of Grill to 200-225 degrees F and preheat with closed lid for 15 minutes.
2. In a bowl, mix together brown sugar, ground espresso, spices, salt and black pepper.
3. Rub the chicken with spice mixture generously.
4. Place the chicken onto the grill and cook for about 3-5 hours.
5. Remove chicken from grill and place onto a cutting board for about 10 minutes before carving.
6. With a sharp knife, cut the chicken into desired-sized pieces and serve.

Nutrition Info: Calories per serving: 540; Carbohydrates: 20.7g; Protein: 88.3g; Fat: 9.6g; Sugar: 18.1g; Sodium: 226mg; Fiber: 1.2g

79. Turkey Legs

Servings: 4
Cooking Time: 5 Hours
Ingredients:
- 4 turkey legs
- For the Brine:
- 1/2 cup curing salt
- 1 tablespoon whole black peppercorns
- 1 cup BBQ rub
- 1/2 cup brown sugar
- 2 bay leaves
- 2 teaspoons liquid smoke
- 16 cups of warm water
- 4 cups ice
- 8 cups of cold water

Directions:
1.   Prepare the brine and for this, take a large stockpot, place it over high heat, pour warm water in it, add peppercorn, bay leaves, and liquid smoke, stir in salt, sugar, and BBQ rub and bring it to a boil.
2.   Remove pot from heat, bring it to room temperature, then pour in cold water, add ice cubes and let the brine chill in the refrigerator.
3.   Then add turkey legs in it, submerge them completely, and let soak for 24 hours in the refrigerator.
4.   After 24 hours, remove turkey legs from the brine, rinse well and pat dry with paper towels.
5.   When ready to cook, switch on the grill, fill the grill hopper with hickory flavored wood pellets, power the grill on by using the control panel, select 'smoke' on the temperature dial, or set the temperature to 250 degrees F and let it preheat for a minimum of 15 minutes.
6.   When the grill has preheated, open the lid, place turkey legs on the grill grate, shut the grill, and smoke for 5 hours until nicely browned and the internal temperature reaches 165 degrees F.
7.   Serve immediately.
Nutrition Info: Calories: 416 Cal ;Fat: 13.3 g ;Carbs: 0 g ;Protein: 69.8 g ;Fiber: 0 g

80.   Succulent Duck Breast

Servings: 4
Cooking Time: 10 Minutes
Ingredients:
- 4 (6-oz.) boneless duck breasts
- 2 tbsp. chicken rub

Directions:
1.   Set the temperature of Grill to 275 degrees F and preheat with closed lid for 15 minutes.
2.   With a sharp knife, score the skin of the duck into ¼-inch diamond pattern.
3.   Season the duck breast with rub evenly.
4.   Place the duck breasts onto the grill, meat side down and cook for about 10 minutes.
5.   Now, set the temperature of Grill to 400 degrees F.
6.   Now, arrange the breasts, skin side down and cook for about 10 minutes, flipping once halfway through.
7.   Remove from the grill and serve.
Nutrition Info: Calories per serving: 231; Carbohydrates: 1.5g; Protein: 37.4g; Fat: 6.8g; Sugar: 0g; Sodium: 233mg; Fiber: 0g

81.　　Lemon Chicken Breast

Servings: 4
Cooking Time: 30 Minutes
Ingredients:
- 6 chicken breasts, skinless and boneless
- ½ cup oil
- 1-3 fresh thyme sprigs
- 1teaspoon ground black pepper
- 2teaspoon salt
- 2teaspoons honey
- 1garlic clove, chopped
- 1lemon, juiced and zested
- Lemon wedges

Directions:
1. Take a bowl and prepare the marinade by mixing thyme, pepper, salt, honey, garlic, lemon zest, and juice. Mix well until dissolved
2. Add oil and whisk
3. Clean breasts and pat them dry, place in a bag alongside marinade and let them sit in the fridge for 4 hours
4. Preheat your smoker to 400 degrees F
5. Drain chicken and smoke until the internal temperature reaches 165 degrees, for about 15 minutes
6. Serve and enjoy!
Nutrition Info: Calories: 230 Fats: 7g Carbs: 1g Fiber: 2g

82.　　Beer Can Chicken

Servings: 6
Cooking Time: 1 Hour And 15 Minutes
Ingredients:
- 5-pound chicken
- 1/2 cup dry chicken rub
- 1 can beer

Directions:
1. Preheat your wood pellet grill on smoke for 5 minutes with the lid open.
2. The lid must then be closed and then preheated up to 450 degrees Fahrenheit
3. Pour out half of the beer then shove the can in the chicken and use the legs like a tripod.
4. Place the chicken on the grill until the internal temperature reaches 165°F.
5. Remove from the grill and let rest for 20 minutes before serving. Enjoy.
Nutrition Info: Calories: 882 Cal Fat: 51 g Carbohydrates: 2 g Protein: 94 g Fiber: 0 g

83.　　Chicken Tenders

Servings: 2 To 4
Cooking Time: 1 Hour, 20 Minutes
Ingredients:
- 1 pound boneless, skinless chicken breast tenders
- 1 batch Chicken Rub

Directions:
1. Supply your smoker with wood pellets and follow the manufacturer's specific start-up procedure. Preheat the grill, with the lid closed, to 180°F.
2. Season the chicken tenders with the rub. Using your hands, work the rub into the meat.
3. Place the tenders directly on the grill grate and smoke for 1 hour.
4. Increase the grill's temperature to 300°F and continue to cook until the tenders' internal temperature reaches 170°F. Remove the tenders from the grill and serve immediately.

84.   Applewood-smoked Whole Turkey

Servings: 6 To 8
Cooking Time: 5 To 6 Hours
Ingredients:
- 1 (10- to 12-pound) turkey, giblets removed
- Extra-virgin olive oil, for rubbing
- ¼ cup poultry seasoning
- 8 tablespoons (1 stick) unsalted butter, melted
- ½ cup apple juice
- 2 teaspoons dried sage
- 2 teaspoons dried thyme

Directions:
1. Supply your smoker with wood pellets and follow the manufacturer's specific start-up procedure. Preheat, with the lid closed, to 250°F.
2. Rub the turkey with oil and season with the poultry seasoning inside and out, getting under the skin.
3. In a bowl, combine the melted butter, apple juice, sage, and thyme to use for basting.
4. Put the turkey in a roasting pan, place on the grill, close the lid, and grill for 5 to 6 hours, basting every hour, until the skin is brown and crispy, or until a meat thermometer inserted in the thickest part of the thigh reads 165°F.
5. Let the bird rest for 15 to 20 minutes before carving.

85.   Spatchcocked Turkey

Servings: 10 To 14
Cooking Time: 2 Hours
Ingredients:
- 1 whole turkey
- 2 tablespoons olive oil
- 1 batch Chicken Rub

Directions:
1. Supply your smoker with wood pellets and follow the manufacturer's specific start-up procedure. Preheat the grill, with the lid closed, to 350°F.
2. To remove the turkey's backbone, place the turkey on a work surface, on its breast. Using kitchen shears, cut along one side of the turkey's backbone and then the other. Pull out the bone.
3. Once the backbone is removed, turn the turkey breast-side up and flatten it.
4. Coat the turkey with olive oil and season it on both sides with the rub. Using your hands, work the rub into the meat and skin.
5. Place the turkey directly on the grill grate, breast-side up, and cook until its internal temperature reaches 170°F.
6. Remove the turkey from the grill and let it rest for 10 minutes, before carving and serving.

86. Garlic Parmesan Chicken Wings

Servings: 6
Cooking Time: 20 Minutes
Ingredients:
- 5 pounds of chicken wings
- 1/2 cup chicken rub
- 3 tablespoons chopped parsley
- 1 cup shredded parmesan cheese
- For the Sauce:
- 5 teaspoons minced garlic
- 2 tablespoons chicken rub
- 1 cup butter, unsalted

Directions:
1.   Switch on the grill, fill the grill hopper with cherry flavored wood pellets, power the grill on by using the control panel, select 'smoke' on the temperature dial, or set the temperature to 450 degrees F and let it preheat for a minimum of 15 minutes.
2.   Meanwhile, take a large bowl, place chicken wings in it, sprinkle with chicken rub and toss until well coated.
3.   When the grill has preheated, open the lid, place chicken wings on the grill grate, shut the grill, and smoke for 10 minutes per side until the internal temperature reaches 165 degrees F.
4.   Meanwhile, prepare the sauce and for this, take a medium saucepan, place it over medium heat, add all the ingredients for the sauce in it and cook for 10 minutes until smooth, set aside until required.
5.   When done, transfer chicken wings to a dish, top with prepared sauce, toss until mixed, garnish with cheese and parsley and then serve.
Nutrition Info: Calories: 180 Cal ;Fat: 1 g ;Carbs: 8 g ;Protein: 0 g ;Fiber: 0 g

87. Trager Smoked Spatchcock Turkey

Servings: 8
Cooking Time: 1 Hour 15 Minutes;
Ingredients:
- 1 turkey
- 1/2 cup melted butter
- 1/4 cup chicken rub
- 1 tbsp onion powder
- 1 tbsp garlic powder
- 1 tbsp rubbed sage

Directions:
1.   Preheat your to high temperature.
2.   Place the turkey on a chopping board with the breast side down and the legs pointing towards you.
3.   Cut either side of the turkey backbone, to remove the spine. Flip the turkey and place it on a pan
4.   Season both sides with the seasonings and place it on the grill skin side up on the grill.
5.   Cook for 30 minutes, reduce temperature, and cook for 45 more minutes or until the internal temperature reaches 165F.
6.   Remove from the and let rest for 15 minutes before slicing and serving.
Nutrition Info: Calories 156, Total fat 16g, Saturated fat 2g, Total carbs 1g, Net carbs 1g Protein 2g, Sugars 0g, Fiber 0g, Sodium 19mg

88.   Bbq Sauce Smothered Chicken Breasts

Servings: 4
Cooking Time: 30 Minutes
Ingredients:
- 1 tsp. garlic, crushed
- ¼ C. olive oil
- 1 tbsp. Worcestershire sauce
- 1 tbsp. sweet mesquite seasoning
- 4 chicken breasts
- 2 tbsp. regular BBQ sauce
- 2 tbsp. spicy BBQ sauce
- 2 tbsp. honey bourbon BBQ sauce

Directions:
1. Set the temperature of Grill to 450 degrees F and preheat with closed lid for 15 minutes.
2. In a large bowl, mix together garlic, oil, Worcestershire sauce and mesquite seasoning.
3. Coat chicken breasts with seasoning mixture evenly.
4. Place the chicken breasts onto the grill and cook for about 20-30 minutes.
5. Meanwhile, in a bowl, mix together all 3 BBQ sauces.
6. In the last 4-5 minutes of cooking, coat breast with BBQ sauce mixture.
7. Serve hot.

Nutrition Info: Calories per serving: 421; Carbohydrates: 10.1g; Protein: 41,2g; Fat: 23.3g; Sugar: 6.9g; Sodium: 763mg; Fiber: 0.2g

89.   Grilled Buffalo Chicken Legs

Servings: 8
Cooking Time: 1 Hour 15 Minutes;
Ingredients:
- 12 chicken legs
- 1/2 tbsp salt
- 1 tbsp buffalo seasoning
- 1 cup Buffalo sauce

Directions:
1. Preheat your to 325F.
2. Toss the chicken legs in salt and seasoning then place them on the preheated grill.
3. Grill for 40 minutes turning twice through the cooking.
4. Increase the heat and cook for 10 more minutes. Brush the chicken legs and brush with buffalo sauce. Cook for an additional 10 minutes or until the internal temperature reaches 165F.
5. Remove from the and brush with more buffalo sauce.
6. Serve with blue cheese, celery, and hot ranch.

Nutrition Info: Calories 956, Total fat 47g, Saturated fat 13g, Total carbs 1g, Net carbs 1g Protein 124g, Sugars 0g, Fiber 0g, Sodium 1750mg

90.   Grilled Chicken

Servings: 6
Cooking Time: 1 Hour 10 Minutes;
Ingredients:
- 5 lb. whole chicken
- 1/2 cup oil
- chicken rub

Directions:
1. Preheat the on the smoke setting with the lid open for 5 minutes. Close the lid and let it heat for 15 minutes or until it reaches 450..
2. Use bakers twine to tie the chicken legs together then rub it with oil. Coat the chicken with the rub and place it on the grill.
3. Grill for 70 minutes with the lid closed or until it reaches an internal temperature of 165F.
4. Remove the chicken from the and let rest for 15 minutes. Cut and serve.

Nutrition Info: Calories 935, Total fat 53g, Saturated fat 15g, Total carbs 0g, Net carbs 0g Protein 107g, Sugars 0g, Fiber 0g, Sodium 320mg

91.   Hickory Smoked Chicken

Servings: 4
Cooking Time: 30 Minutes
Ingredients:
- 4 chicken breasts
- ¼ cup olive oil
- 1 teaspoon pressed garlic
- 1 tablespoon Worcestershire sauce
- Kirkland Sweet Mesquite Seasoning as needed
- 1 button Honey Bourbon Sauce

Directions:
1.   Place all ingredients in a bowl except for the Bourbon sauce. Massage the chicken until all parts are coated with the seasoning.
2.   Allow to marinate in the fridge for 4 hours.
3.   Once ready to cook, fire the Grill to 350F. Use Hickory wood pellets and close the lid. Preheat for 15 minutes.
4.   Place the chicken directly into the grill grate and cook for 30 minutes. Flip the chicken halfway through the cooking time.
5.   Five minutes before the cooking time ends, brush all surfaces of the chicken with the Honey Bourbon Sauce.
6.   Serve immediately.

Nutrition Info: Calories per serving: 622; Protein: 60.5g; Carbs: 1.1g; Fat: 40.3g Sugar: 0.4g

92.   Smoked Chicken And Potatoes

Servings: 4
Cooking Time: 1 Hour And 30 Minutes
Ingredients:
- 1 2.5-pounds rotisserie chicken
- 2 tablespoon coconut sugar
- 1 tablespoons onion powder
- 2 tablespoon garlic powder
- 1 teaspoon cayenne pepper powder
- 2 teaspoon kosher salt
- 4 tablespoons olive oil
- 2 pounds creamer potatoes, scrubbed and halved
- A dash of black pepper powder

Directions:
1.   Place the chicken in a bowl. In a smaller bowl, combine the coconut sugar, onion powder, garlic powder, cayenne pepper powder, and salt. Add in the olive oil. Rub the mixture into the chicken and allow to marinate for 4 hours in the fridge.
2.   Fire the Grill to 400F and close the lid. Preheat to 15 minutes.
3.   Place the seasoned chicken in a heat-proof dish and place the potatoes around the chicken. Season the potatoes with salt.
4.   Place in the grill and cook for 30 minutes. Lower the heat to 250F and cook for another hour.
5.   Insert a meat thermometer in the thickest part of the chicken and make sure that the temperature reads at 165F. Flip the chicken halfway through the cooking time for even browning.

Nutrition Info: Calories per serving: 991; Protein: 79.7g; Carbs: 49.8g; Fat: 73.6g Sugar: 6.5g

93. Wood Pellet Grilled Chicken Kabobs

Servings: 6
Cooking Time: 12 Minutes
Ingredients:
- 1/2 cup olive oil
- 2 tbsp white vinegar
- 1 tbsp lemon juice
- 1-1/2 tbsp salt
- 1/2 tbsp pepper, coarsely ground
- 2 tbsp chives, freshly chopped
- 1-1/2 tbsp thyme, freshly chopped
- 2 tbsp Italian parsley freshly chopped
- 1tbsp garlic, minced
- Kabobs
- 1 each orange, red, and yellow pepper
- 1-1/2 pounds chicken breast, boneless and skinless
- 12 mini mushrooms

Directions:
1. In a mixing bowl, add all the marinade ingredients and mix well. Toss the chicken and mushrooms in the marinade then refrigerate for 30 minutes.
2. Meanwhile, soak the skewers in hot water. Remove the chicken from the fridge and start assembling the kabobs.
3. Preheat your wood pellet to 450°F.
4. Grill the kabobs in the wood pellet for 6 minutes, flip them and grill for 6 more minutes.
5. Remove from the grill and let rest. Heat up the naan bread on the grill for 2 minutes.
6. Serve and enjoy.
Nutrition Info: Calories: 165 Cal Fat: 13 g Carbohydrates: 1 g   Protein: 33 g Fiber: 0 g

94.   Wood Pellet Grilled Buffalo Chicken

Servings: 6
Cooking Time: 20 Minutes
Ingredients:
- 5 chicken breasts, boneless and skinless
- 2 tbsp homemade barbeque rub
- 1 cup homemade Cholula buffalo sauce

Directions:
1. Preheat the wood pellet grill to 400°F.
2. Slice the chicken into long strips and season with barbeque rub.
3. Place the chicken on the grill and paint both sides with buffalo sauce.
4. Cook for 4 minutes with the grill closed. Cook while flipping and painting with buffalo sauce every 5 minutes until the internal temperature reaches 165°F.
5. Remove from the grill and serve when warm. Enjoy.
Nutrition Info: Calories: 176 Cal Fat: 4 g Carbohydrates: 1 g   Protein: 32 g Fiber: 0 g

95.   Chicken Breast

Servings: 6
Cooking Time: 15 Minutes
Ingredients:
- 3 chicken breasts
- 1 tbsp avocado oil
- 1/4 tbsp garlic powder
- 1/4 tbsp onion powder
- 3/4 tbsp salt
- 1/4 tbsp pepper

Directions:
1. Preheat your to 375F
2. Cut the chicken breast into halves lengthwise then coat with avocado oil.
3. Season with garlic powder, onion powder, salt, and pepper.
4. Place the chicken on the grill and cook for 7 minutes on each side or until the internal temperature reaches 165F

Nutrition Info: Calories 120, Total fat 4g, Saturated fat 1g, Total carbs 0g, Net carbs 0g Protein 19g, Sugars 0g, Fiber 0g, Sodium 309mg

96.   Asian Miso Chicken Wings

Servings: 6
Cooking Time: 25 Minutes
Ingredients:
- 2 lb chicken wings
- 3/4 cup soy
- 1/2 cup pineapple juice
- 1 tbsp sriracha
- 1/8 cup miso
- 1/8 cup gochujang
- 1/2 cup water
- 1/2 cup oil
- Togarashi

Directions:
1. Preheat the to 375F
2. Combine all the ingredients except togarashi in a zip lock bag. Toss until the chicken wings are well coated. Refrigerate for 12 hours
3. Pace the wings on the grill grates and close the lid. Cook for 25 minutes or until the internal temperature reaches 165F
4. Remove the wings from the and sprinkle Togarashi.
5. Serve when hot and enjoy.

Nutrition Info: Calories 703, Total fat 56g, Saturated fat 14g, Total carbs 24g, Net carbs 23g Protein 27g, Sugars 6g, Fiber 1g, Sodium 1156mg

97. Christmas Dinner Goose

Servings: 12
Cooking Time: 3 Hours
Ingredients:
- 1½ C. kosher salt
- 1 C. brown sugar
- 20 C. water
- 1 (12-lb.) whole goose, giblets removed
- 1 naval orange, cut into 6 wedges
- 1 large onion, cut into 8 wedges
- 2 bay leaves
- ¼ C. juniper berries, crushed
- 12 black peppercorns
- Salt and freshly ground black pepper, to taste
- 1 apple, cut into 6 wedges
- 2-3 fresh parsley sprigs

Directions:
1. Trim off any loose neck skin.
2. Then, trim the first two joints off the wings.
3. Wash the goose under cold running water and with paper towels, pat dry it.
4. With the tip of a paring knife, prick the goose all over the skin.
5. In a large pitcher, dissolve kosher salt and brown sugar in water.
6. Squeeze 3 orange wedges into brine.
7. Add goose, 4 onion wedges, bay leaves, juniper berries and peppercorns in brine and refrigerate for 24 hours.
8. Set the temperature of Grill to 350 degrees F and preheat with closed lid for 15 minutes.
9. Remove the goose from brine and with paper towels, pat dry completely.
10. Season the in and outside of goose with salt and black pepper evenly.
11. Stuff the cavity with apple wedges, herbs, remaining orange and onion wedges.
12. With kitchen strings, tie the legs together loosely.
13. Place the goose onto a rack arranged in a shallow roasting pan.
14. Arrange the goose on grill and cook for about 1 hour.
15. With a basting bulb, remove some of the fat from the pan and cook for about 1 hour.
16. Again, remove excess fat from the pan and cook for about ½-1 hour more.
17. Remove goose from grill and place onto a cutting board for about 20 minutes before carving.
18. With a sharp knife, cut the goose into desired-sized pieces and serve.

Nutrition Info: Calories per serving: 907; Carbohydrates: 23.5g; Protein: 5.6g; Fat: 60.3g; Sugar: 19.9g; Sodium: 8000mg; Fiber: 1.1g

98. Cajun Chicken Breasts

Servings: 6
Cooking Time: 6 Hours
Ingredients:
- 2 lb. skinless, boneless chicken breasts
- 2 tbsp. Cajun seasoning
- 1 C. BBQ sauce

Directions:
1. Set the temperature of Grill to 225 degrees F and preheat with closed lid for 15 minutes.
2. Rub the chicken breasts with Cajun seasoning generously.
3. Place the chicken breasts onto the grill and cook for about 4-6 hours.
4. During last hour of cooking, coat the breasts with BBQ sauce twice.
5. Serve hot.

Nutrition Info: Calories per serving: 252; Carbohydrates: 15.1g; Protein: 33.8g; Fat: 5.5g; Sugar: 10.9g; Sodium: 570mg; Fiber: 0.3g

99.   Chicken Tikka Masala

Servings: 4
Cooking Time: 1 Hour

Ingredients:

- 1 tablespoon garam masala
- 1 tablespoon smoked paprika
- 1 tablespoon ground coriander
- 1 tablespoon ground cumin
- 1 teaspoon ground cayenne pepper
- 1 teaspoon turmeric
- 1 onion, sliced
- 6 cloves garlic, minced
- 1/4 cup olive oil
- 1 tablespoon ginger, chopped
- 1 tablespoon lemon juice
- 1 1/2 cups Greek yogurt
- 1 tablespoon lime juice
- 1 tablespoon curry powder
- Salt to taste
- 1 tablespoon lime juice
- 12 chicken drumsticks
- Chopped cilantro

Directions:

1. Make the marinade by mixing all the spices, onion, garlic, olive oil, ginger, lemon juice, yogurt, lime juice, curry powder and salt.
2. Transfer to a food processor.
3. Pulse until smooth.
4. Divide the mixture into two.
5. Marinade the chicken in the first bowl.
6. Cover the bowl and refrigerate for 12 hours.
7. Set the wood pellet grill to high.
8. Preheat it for 15 minutes while the lid is closed.
9. Grill the chicken for 50 minutes.
10. Garnish with the chopped cilantro.
11. Tips: You can also smoke the chicken before grilling.

100. Rosemary Orange Chicken

Servings: 6
Cooking Time: 45 Minutes
Ingredients:
- 4 pounds chicken, backbone removed
- For the Marinade:
- 2 teaspoons salt
- 3 tablespoons chopped rosemary leaves
- 2 teaspoons Dijon mustard
- 1 orange, zested
- 1/4 cup olive oil
- ¼ cup of orange juice

Directions:
1. Prepare the chicken and for this, rinse the chicken, pat dry with paper towels and then place in a large baking dish.
2. Prepare the marinade and for this, take a medium bowl, place all of its ingredients in it and whisk until combined.
3. Cover chicken with the prepared marinade, cover with a plastic wrap, and then marinate for a minimum of 2 hours in the refrigerator, turning halfway.
4. When ready to cook, switch on the grill, fill the grill hopper with flavored wood pellets, power the grill on by using the control panel, select 'smoke' on the temperature dial, or set the temperature to 350 degrees F and let it preheat for a minimum of 5 minutes.
5. When the grill has preheated, open the lid, place chicken on the grill grate skin-side down, shut the grill and smoke for 45 minutes until well browned, and the internal temperature reaches 165 degrees F.
6. When done, transfer chicken to a cutting board, let it rest for 10 minutes, cut it into slices, and then serve.

Nutrition Info: Calories: 258 Cal ;Fat: 17.4 g ;Carbs: 5.2 g ;Protein: 19.3 g ;Fiber: 0.3 g

101. Smoked Cornish Hens

Servings: 6
Cooking Time: 1 Hour
Ingredients:
- 6 Cornish hens
- 3 tbsp canola oil
- 6 tbsp rub

Directions:
1. Preheat your to 275F.
2. Meanwhile, rub the hens with canola oil then with your favorite rub.
3. Place the hens on the grill with the breast side down. Smoke for 30 minutes.
4. Flip the hens and increase the temperature to 400F. Cook until the internal temperature reaches 165F.
5. Remove the hens from the grill and let rest for 10 minutes before serving.

Nutrition Info: Calories 696, Total fat 50g, Saturated fat 13g, Total carbs 1g, Net carbs 1g Protein 57g, Sugars 0g, Fiber 0g, Sodium 165mg

102. Smoked Chicken With Apricot Bbq Glaze

Servings: 6
Cooking Time: 30 Minutes
Ingredients:
- 2 whole chicken, halved
- 4 tablespoon Chicken Rub
- 1 cup Trager Apricot BBQ Sauce

Directions:
1. Massage the chicken with the chicken rub. Allow to marinate for 2 hours in the fridge.
2. When ready to cook, fire the Grill to 350F. Use preferred wood pellets. Close the grill lid and preheat for 15 minutes.
3. Place the chicken on the grill grate and grill for 15 minutes on each side. Baste the chicken with Apricot BBQ glaze.
4. Once cooked, allow to rest for 10 minutes before slicing.

Nutrition Info: Calories per serving: 304; Protein: 49g; Carbs: 10.2g; Fat: 6.5g Sugar: 8.7g

103. Chile Lime Chicken

Servings: 1
Cooking Time: 15 Minutes
Ingredients:
- 1 chicken breast
- 1 tbsp oil
- 1 tbsp spiceology Chile Lime Seasoning

Directions:
1. Preheat your to 400F.
2. Brush the chicken breast with oil then sprinkle the chile-lime seasoning and salt.
3. Place the chicken breast on the grill and cook for 7 minutes on each side or until the internal temperature reaches 165F.
4. Serve when hot and enjoy.

Nutrition Info: Calories 131, Total fat 5g, Saturated fat 1g, Total carbs 4g, Net carbs 3g Protein 19g, Sugars 1g, Fiber 1g, Sodium 235mg

104. Chicken Cordon Bleu

Servings: 6
Cooking Time: 40 Minutes

Ingredients:

- 6 boneless skinless chicken breasts
- 6 slices of ham
- 12 slices swiss cheese
- 1cup panko breadcrumbs
- ½ cup all-purpose flour
- 1tsp ground black pepper or to taste
- 1tsp salt or to taste
- 4tbsp grated parmesan cheese
- 2tbsp melted butter
- ½ tsp garlic powder
- ½ tsp thyme
- ¼ tsp parsley

Directions:

1. Butterfly the chicken breast with a pairing knife. Place the chicken breast in between 2 plastic wraps and pound with a mallet until the chicken breasts are ¼ inch thick.
2. Place a plastic wrap on a flat surface. Place one fat chicken breast on it.
3. Place one slice of swiss cheese on the chicken. Place one slice of ham over the cheese and place another cheese slice over the ham.
4. Roll the chicken breast tightly. Fold both ends of the roll tightly. Pin both ends of the rolled chicken breast with a toothpick.
5. Repeat step 3 and 4 for the remaining chicken breasts
6. In a mixing bowl, combine the all-purpose flour, ½ tsp salt, and ½ tsp pepper. Set aside.
7. In another mixing bowl, combine breadcrumbs, parmesan, butter, garlic, thyme, parsley, ½ tsp salt, and ½ tsp pepper. Set aside.
8. Break the eggs into another mixing bowl and whisk. Set aside.
9. Grease a baking sheet.
10. Bake one chicken breast roll. Dip into the flour mixture, brush with eggs and dip into breadcrumb mixture. The chicken breast should be coated.
11. Place it on the baking sheet.
12. Repeat steps 9 and 10 for the remaining breast rolls.
13. Preheat your grill to 375°F with the lid closed for 15 minutes.
14. Place the baking sheet on the grill and cook for about 40 minutes, or until the chicken is golden brown.
15. Remove the baking sheet from the grill and let the chicken rest for a few minutes.
16. Slice cordon bleu and serve.

Nutrition Info: Calories: 560 Total Fat: 27.4 g Saturated Fat: 15.9 g Cholesterol: 156mg Sodium: 1158 mg Total Carbohydrate: 23.2 g Dietary Fiber: 1.1 g Total Sugars: 1.2 g Protein: 54.3 g

105. Sheet Pan Chicken Fajitas

Servings: 10
Cooking Time: 10 Minutes
Ingredients:
- 2 lb chicken breast
- 1 onion, sliced
- 1 red bell pepper, seeded and sliced
- 1 orange-red bell pepper, seeded and sliced
- 1 tbsp salt
- 1/2 tbsp onion powder
- 1/2 tbsp granulated garlic
- 2 tbsp Spiceologist Chile Margarita Seasoning
- 2 tbsp oil

Directions:
1. Preheat the to 450F and line a baking sheet with parchment paper.
2. In a mixing bowl, combine seasonings and oil then toss with the peppers and chicken.
3. Place the baking sheet in the and let heat for 10 minutes with the lid closed.
4. Open the lid and place the veggies and the chicken in a single layer. Close the lid and cook for 10 minutes or until the chicken is no longer pink.
5. Serve with warm tortillas and top with your favorite toppings.

Nutrition Info: Calories 211, Total fat 6g, Saturated fat 1g, Total carbs 5g, Net carbs 4g Protein 29g, Sugars 4g, Fiber 1g, Sodium 360mg

106. Lemon Chicken Breasts

Servings: 6
Cooking Time: 40 Minutes
Ingredients:
- 1 clove of garlic, minced
- 2 teaspoons honey
- 2 teaspoons salt
- 1 teaspoon black pepper, ground
- 2 sprigs fresh thyme leaves
- 1 lemon, zested and juiced
- ½ cup olive oil
- 6 boneless chicken breasts

Directions:
1. Make the marinade by combining the garlic, honey, salt, pepper, thyme, lemon zest, and juice in a bowl. Whisk until well-combined.
2. Place the chicken into the marinade and mix with hands to coat the meat with the marinade. Refrigerate for 4 hours.
3. When ready to grill, fire the Grill to 400F. Close the lid and preheat for 10 minutes.
4. Drain the chicken and discard the marinade.
5. Arrange the chicken breasts directly on to the grill grate and cook for 40 minutes or until the internal temperature of the thickest part of the chicken reaches to 165F.
6. Drizzle with more lemon juice before serving.

Nutrition Info: Calories per serving: 669; Protein: 60.6g; Carbs: 3g; Fat: 44.9g Sugar: 2.1g

107. Grill Bbq Chicken Breasts

Servings: 4
Cooking Time: 30 Minutes
Ingredients:
- 4 whole chicken breasts, deboned
- ¼ cup olive oil
- 1 teaspoon pressed garlic
- 1 teaspoon Worcestershire sauce
- 1 teaspoon cayenne pepper powder
- ½ cup 'Que BBQ Sauce

Directions:
1. In a bowl, combine all ingredients except for the 'Que BBQ Sauce and make sure to rub the chicken breasts until coated with the mixture. Allow to marinate in the fridge for at least overnight.
2. Place the preferred wood pellets into the Grill and fire the grill. Allow the temperature to rise to 500F and preheat for 5 minutes. Reduce the temperature to 165F.
3. Place the chicken on the grill grate and cook for 30 minutes.
4. Five minutes before the chicken is done, glaze the chicken with Traeger's BBQ sauce.
5. Serve immediately.

Nutrition Info: Calories per serving: 631; Protein: 61g; Carbs: 2.9g; Fat: 40.5g Sugar: 1.5g

108. Budget Friendly Chicken Legs

Servings: 6
Cooking Time: 1½ Hours
Ingredients:
- For Brine:
- 1 C. kosher salt
- ¾ C. light brown sugar
- 16 C. water
- 6 chicken leg quarters
- For Glaze:
- ½ C. mayonnaise
- 2 tbsp. BBQ rub
- 2 tbsp. fresh chives, minced
- 1 tbsp. garlic, minced

Directions:
1. For brine: in a bucket, dissolve salt and brown sugar in water.
2. Place the chicken quarters in brine and refrigerate, covered for about 4 hours.
3. Set the temperature of Grill to 275 degrees F and preheat with closed lid for 15 minutes.
4. Remove chicken quarters from brine and rinse under cold running water.
5. With paper towels, pat dry chicken quarters.
6. For glaze: in a bowl, add all ingredients and mix till ell combined.
7. Coat chicken quarters with glaze evenly.
8. Place the chicken leg quarters onto grill and cook for about 1-1½ hours.
9. Serve immediately.

Nutrition Info: Calories per serving: 399; Carbohydrates: 17.2g; Protein: 29.1g; Fat: 24.7g; Sugar: 14.2g; Sodium: 15000mg; Fiber: 0g

109.   Smoked Airline Chicken

Servings: 4
Cooking Time: 1 To 2 Hours
Ingredients:
- 2 boneless chicken breasts with drumettes attached
- ½ cup soy sauce
- ½ cup teriyaki sauce
- ¼ cup canola oil
- ¼ cup white vinegar
- 1 tablespoon minced garlic
- ¼ cup chopped scallions
- 2 teaspoons freshly ground black pepper
- 1 teaspoon ground mustard

Directions:
1. Place the chicken in a baking dish.
2. In a bowl, whisk together the soy sauce, teriyaki sauce, canola oil, vinegar, garlic, scallions, pepper and ground mustard, then pour this marinade over the chicken, coating both sides.
3. Refrigerate the chicken in marinade for 4 hours, turning over every hour.
4. When ready to smoke the chicken, supply your smoker with wood pellets and follow the manufacturer's specific start-up procedure. Preheat, with the lid closed, to 250°F.
5. Remove the chicken from the marinade but do not rinse. Discard the marinade.
6. Arrange the chicken directly on the grill, close the lid, and smoke for 1 hour 30 minutes to 2 hours, or until a meat thermometer inserted in the thickest part of the meat reads 165°F.
7. Let the meat rest for 3 minutes before serving.

110.   Hickory Smoked Chicken Leg And Thigh Quarters

Servings: 6
Cooking Time: 2 Hours
Ingredients:
- 6 chicken legs (with thigh and drumsticks)
- 2 tablespoons olive oil
- Poultry Rub to taste

Directions:
1. Place all ingredients in a bowl and mix until the chicken pieces are coated in oil and rub. Allow to marinate for at least 2 hours.
2. Fire the Grill to 180F. Close the lid and allow to preheat for 10 minutes. Use hickory wood pellets to smoke your chicken.
3. Arrange the chicken on the grill grate and smoke for one hour. Increase the temperature to 350F and continue cooking for another hour until the chicken is golden and the juices run clean.
4. To check if the meat is cooked, insert a meat thermometer, and make sure that the temperature on the thickest part of the chicken registers at 165F.
5. Remove the chicken and serve.

Nutrition Info: Calories per serving: 358 ; Protein: 50.8g; Carbs: 0g; Fat: 15.7g Sugar:0 g

111.   Bourbon Bbq Smoked Chicken Wings

Servings: 8
Cooking Time: 24 Minutes
Ingredients:
- 4 pounds chicken wings, patted dry
- 2 tablespoons olive oil
- Salt and pepper to taste
- ½ medium yellow onions, minced
- 5 cloves garlic, mince
- ½ cup bourbon
- 2 cups ketchup
- 1/3 cup apple cider vinegar
- 2 tablespoons liquid smoke
- ½ teaspoon kosher salt
- ½ teaspoon black pepper
- A dash of hot sauce

Directions:
1. Place the chicken in a bowl and drizzle with olive oil. Season with salt and pepper to taste. In another bowl, combine the rest of the ingredients and set aside.
2. Fire the Grill to 400F. Use hickory wood pellets. Close the lid and allow to preheat for 15 minutes.
3. Place the chicken on the grill grate and cook for 12 minutes on each side.
4. Using a brush, brush the chicken wings with bourbon sauce on all sides.
5. Flip the chicken and cook for another 12 minutes with the lid closed.

Nutrition Info: Calories per serving: 384 ; Protein: 50.7g; Carbs: 17.8 g; Fat: 11.5g Sugar: 13.1g

112.   Wild West Wings

Servings: 4
Cooking Time: 1 Hour
Ingredients:
- 2 pounds chicken wings
- 2 tablespoons extra-virgin olive oil
- 2 packages ranch dressing mix (such as Hidden Valley brand)
- ¼ cup prepared ranch dressing (optional)

Directions:
1. Supply your smoker with wood pellets and follow the manufacturer's specific start-up procedure. Preheat, with the lid closed, to 350°F.
2. Place the chicken wings in a large bowl and toss with the olive oil and ranch dressing mix.
3. Arrange the wings directly on the grill, or line the grill with aluminum foil for easy cleanup, close the lid, and smoke for 25 minutes.
4. Flip and smoke for 20 to 35 minutes more, or until a meat thermometer inserted in the thickest part of the wings reads 165°F and the wings are crispy. (Note: The wings will likely be done after 45 minutes, but an extra 10 to 15 minutes makes them crispy without drying the meat.)
5. Serve warm with ranch dressing (if using).

Servings: 6
Cooking Time: 1 Hour
Ingredients:
- 3 pounds of chicken wings
- 2 tablespoons olive oil
- For the Brine:
- 1 head garlic, halved
- 1 lemon, halved
- 1/2 cup sugar
- 1 cup of sea salt
- 4 sprigs of thyme
- 10 peppercorns
- 16 cups of water
- For the Sauce:
- 2 teaspoons minced garlic
- 1/2 cup gochujang hot pepper paste
- 1 tablespoon grated ginger
- 2 tablespoons of rice wine vinegar
- 1/3 cup honey
- 1/4 cup soy sauce
- 2 tablespoons lime juice
- 2 tablespoons toasted sesame oil
- 1/4 cup melted butter

Directions:
1. Prepare the brine and for this, take a large stockpot, place it over high heat, pour in water, stir in salt and sugar until dissolved, and bring to a boil.
2. Then remove the pot from heat, add remaining ingredients for the brine, and bring the brine to room temperature.
3. Add chicken wings, submerge them completely, cover the pot and let wings soak for a minimum of 4 hours in the refrigerator.
4. When ready to cook, switch on the grill, fill the grill hopper with flavored wood pellets, power the grill on by using the control panel, select 'smoke' on the temperature dial, or set the temperature to 375 degrees F and let it preheat for a minimum of 15 minutes.
5. Meanwhile, remove chicken wings from the brine, pat dry with paper towels, place them in a large bowl, drizzle with oil and toss until well coated.
6. When the grill has preheated, open the lid, place chicken wings on the grill grate, shut the grill, and smoke for 1 hour until the internal temperature reaches 165 degrees F.
7. Meanwhile, prepare the sauce and for this, take a medium bowl, place all of the sauce ingredients in it and whisk until smooth.
8. When done, transfer chicken wings to a dish, top with prepared sauce, toss until coated, and then serve.
Nutrition Info: Calories: 137 Cal ;Fat: 9 g ;Carbs: 4 g ;Protein: 8 g ;Fiber: 1 g

114. Mini Turducken Roulade

Servings: 6
Cooking Time: 2 Hours

Ingredients:

- 1 (16-ounce) boneless turkey breast
- 1 (8-to 10-ounce) boneless duck breast
- 1 (8-ounce) boneless, skinless chicken breast
- Salt
- Freshly ground black pepper
- 2 cups Italian dressing
- 2 tablespoons Cajun seasoning
- 1 cup prepared seasoned stuffing mix
- 8 slices bacon
- Butcher's string

Directions:

1. Butterfly the turkey, duck, and chicken breasts, cover with plastic wrap and, using a mallet, flatten each ½ inch thick.
2. Season all the meat on both sides with a little salt and pepper.
3. In a medium bowl, combine the Italian dressing and Cajun seasoning. Spread one-fourth of the mixture on top of the flattened turkey breast.
4. Place the duck breast on top of the turkey, spread it with one-fourth of the dressing mixture, and top with the stuffing mix.
5. Place the chicken breast on top of the duck and spread with one-fourth of the dressing mixture.
6. Supply your smoker with wood pellets and follow the manufacturer's specific start-up procedure. Preheat, with the lid closed, to 275°F.
7. Tightly roll up the stack, tie with butcher's string, and slather the whole thing with the remaining dressing mixture.
8. Wrap the bacon slices around the turducken and secure with toothpicks, or try making a bacon weave (see the technique for this in the Jalapeño-Bacon Pork Tenderloin recipe).
9. Place the turducken roulade in a roasting pan. Transfer to the grill, close the lid, and roast for 2 hours, or until a meat thermometer inserted in the turducken reads 165°F. Tent with aluminum foil in the last 30 minutes, if necessary, to keep from overbrowning.
10. Let the turducken rest for 15 to 20 minutes before carving. Serve warm.

115.   Hellfire Chicken Wings

Servings: 6
Cooking Time: 40 Minutes
Ingredients:
- 3 pounds chicken wings, tips removed
- 2 tablespoons olive oil
- For the Rub:
- 1 teaspoon onion powder
- 1 teaspoon salt
- 1 teaspoon garlic powder
- 1 tablespoon paprika
- 1 teaspoon ground black pepper
- 1 teaspoon celery seed
- 1 teaspoon cayenne pepper
- 2 teaspoons brown sugar
- For the Sauce:
- 4 jalapeno peppers, sliced crosswise
- 8 tablespoons butter, unsalted
- 1/2 cup hot sauce
- 1/2 cup cilantro leaves

Directions:
1.   Switch on the grill, fill the grill hopper with hickory flavored wood pellets, power the grill on by using the control panel, select 'smoke' on the temperature dial, or set the temperature to 350 degrees F and let it preheat for a minimum of 15 minutes.
2.   Prepare the chicken wings and for this, remove tips from the wings, cut each chicken wing through the joint into two pieces, and then place in a large bowl.
3.   Prepare the rub and for this, take a small bowl, place all of its ingredients in it and then stir until combined.
4.   Sprinkle prepared rub on the chicken wings and then toss until well coated.
5.   Meanwhile,
6.   When the grill has preheated, open the lid, place chicken wings on the grill grate, shut the grill and smoke for 40 minutes until golden brown and skin have turned crisp, turning halfway.
7.   Meanwhile, prepare the sauce and for this, take a small saucepan, place it over medium-low heat, add butter in it and when it melts, add jalapeno and cook for 4 minutes.
8.   Then stir in hot sauce and cilantro until mixed and remove the pan from heat.
9.   When done, transfer chicken wings to a dish, top with prepared sauce, toss until coated, and then serve.
Nutrition Info: Calories: 250 Cal ;Fat: 15 g ;Carbs: 11 g ;Protein: 19 g ;Fiber: 1 g

116.   Turkey With Apricot Barbecue Glaze

Servings: 4
Cooking Time: 30 Minutes
Ingredients:
- 4 turkey breast fillets
- 4 tablespoons chicken rub
- 1 cup apricot barbecue sauce

Directions:
1.   Preheat the wood pellet grill to 365 degrees F for 15 minutes while the lid is closed.
2.   Season the turkey fillets with the chicken run.
3.   Grill the turkey fillets for 5 minutes per side.
4.   Brush both sides with the barbecue sauce and grill for another 5 minutes per side.
5.   Tips: You can sprinkle turkey with chili powder if you want your dish spicy.

117.   Bbq Half Chickens

Servings: 4
Cooking Time: 75 Minutes
Ingredients:
- 3.5-pound whole chicken, cleaned, halved
- Summer rub as needed
- Apricot BBQ sauce as needed

Directions:
1.   Switch on the grill, fill the grill hopper with apple-flavored wood pellets, power the grill on by using the control panel, select 'smoke' on the temperature dial, or set the temperature to 375 degrees F and let it preheat for a minimum of 15 minutes.
2.   Meanwhile, cut chicken in half along with backbone and then season with summer rub.
3.   When the grill has preheated, open the lid, place chicken halves on the grill grate skin-side up, shut the grill, change the smoking temperature to 225 degrees F, and smoke for 1 hour and 30 minutes until the internal temperature reaches 160 degrees F.
4.   Then brush chicken generously with apricot sauce and continue grilling for 10 minutes until glazed.
5.   When done, transfer chicken to cutting to a dish, let it rest for 5 minutes, and then serve.
Nutrition Info: Calories: 435 Cal ;Fat: 20 g ;Carbs: 20 g ;Protein: 42 g ;Fiber: 1 g

118.   Chicken Wings

Servings: 4
Cooking Time: 15 Minutes
Ingredients:
- Fresh chicken wings
- Salt to taste
- Pepper to taste
- Garlic powder
- Onion powder
- Cayenne
- Paprika
- Seasoning salt
- Barbeque sauce to taste

Directions:
1.   Preheat the wood pellet grill to low. Mix seasoning and coat on chicken. Put the wings on the grill and cook. Place the wings on the grill and cook for 20 minutes or until the wings are fully cooked. Let rest to cool for 5 minutes then toss with barbeque sauce. Serve with orzo and salad. Enjoy.
Nutrition Info: Calories: 311 Cal Fat: 22 g Carbohydrates: 22 g   Protein: 22 g Fiber: 3 g

119.   Maple Turkey Breast

Servings: 4
Cooking Time: 2 Hours
Ingredients:
- 3 tablespoons olive oil
- 3 tablespoons dark brown sugar
- 3 tablespoons garlic, minced
- 2 tablespoons Cajun seasoning
- 2 tablespoons Worcestershire sauce
- 6 lb. turkey breast fillets

Directions:
1.   Combine olive oil, sugar, garlic, Cajun seasoning and Worcestershire sauce in a bowl.
2.   Soak the turkey breast fillets in the marinade.
3.   Cover and marinate for 4 hours.
4.   Grill the turkey at 180 degrees F for 2 hours.
5.   Tips: You can also sprinkle dry rub on the turkey before grilling.

120.   Thanksgiving Dinner Turkey

Servings: 16
Cooking Time: 4 Hours
Ingredients:
- ½ lb. butter, softened
- 2 tbsp. fresh thyme, chopped
- 2 tbsp. fresh rosemary, chopped
- 6 garlic cloves, crushed
- 1 (20-lb.) whole turkey, neck and giblets removed
- Salt and freshly ground black pepper, to taste

Directions:
1. Set the temperature of Grill to 300 degrees F and preheat with closed lid for 15 minutes, using charcoal.
2. In a bowl, place butter, fresh herbs, garlic, salt and black pepper and mix well.
3. With your fingers, separate the turkey skin from breast to create a pocket.
4. Stuff the breast pocket with ¼-inch thick layer of butter mixture.
5. Season the turkey with salt and black pepper evenly.
6. Arrange the turkey onto the grill and cook for 3-4 hours.
7. Remove the turkey from grill and place onto a cutting board for about 15-20 minutes before carving.
8. With a sharp knife, cut the turkey into desired-sized pieces and serve.

Nutrition Info: Calories per serving: 965; Carbohydrates: 0.6g; Protein: 106.5g; Fat: 52g; Sugar: 0g; Sodium: 1916mg; Fiber: 0.2g

121.   Buttered Thanksgiving Turkey

Servings: 12 To 14
Cooking Time: 5 To 6 Hours
Ingredients:
- 1 whole turkey (make sure the turkey is not pre-brined)
- 2 batches Garlic Butter Injectable
- 3 tablespoons olive oil
- 1 batch Chicken Rub
- 2 tablespoons butter

Directions:
1.   Supply your smoker with wood pellets and follow the manufacturer's specific start-up procedure. Preheat the grill, with the lid closed, to 180°F.
2.   Inject the turkey throughout with the garlic butter injectable. Coat the turkey with olive oil and season it with the rub. Using your hands, work the rub into the meat and skin.
3.   Place the turkey directly on the grill grate and smoke for 3 or 4 hours (for an 8- to 12-pound turkey, cook for 3 hours; for a turkey over 12 pounds, cook for 4 hours), basting it with butter every hour.
4.   Increase the grill's temperature to 375°F and continue to cook until the turkey's internal temperature reaches 170°F.
5.   Remove the turkey from the grill and let it rest for 10 minutes, before carving and serving.

122. Roasted Chicken With Pimenton Potatoes

Servings: 16
Cooking Time: 1 Hour
Ingredients:

- 2 whole chicken
- 6 clove garlic, minced
- 2 tablespoons salt
- 3 tablespoons pimento (smoked paprika)
- 3 tablespoons extra virgin olive oil
- 2 bunch fresh thyme
- 3 pounds Yukon gold potatoes

Directions:
1. Season the whole chicken with garlic, salt, paprika, olive oil, and thyme. Massage the chicken to coat all surface of the chicken with the spices. Tie the legs together with a string. Place in a baking dish and place the potatoes on the side. Season the potatoes with salt and olive oil.
2. Allow the chicken to rest in the fridge for 4 hours.
3. When ready to cook, fire the Grill to 300F. Use preferred wood pellets. Close the grill lid and preheat for 15 minutes.
4. Place the chicken and potatoes in the grill and cook for 1 hour until a thermometer inserted in the thickest part of the chicken comes out clean.
5. Remove from the grill and allow to rest before carving.

Nutrition Info: Calories per serving: 210; Protein: 26.1g; Carbs: 15.3g; Fat: 4.4g Sugar: 0.7g

123. Paprika Chicken

Servings: 7
Cooking Time: 2 – 4 Hours
Ingredients:

- 4-6 chicken breast
- 4 tablespoons olive oil
- 2tablespoons smoked paprika
- ½ tablespoon salt
- ¼ teaspoon pepper
- 2teaspoons garlic powder
- 2teaspoons garlic salt
- 2teaspoons pepper
- 1teaspoon cayenne pepper
- 1teaspoon rosemary

Directions:
1. Preheat your smoker to 220 degrees Fahrenheit using your favorite wood Pellets
2. Prepare your chicken breast according to your desired shapes and transfer to a greased baking dish
3. Take a medium bowl and add spices, stir well
4. Press the spice mix over chicken and transfer the chicken to smoker
5. Smoke for 1-1 and a ½ hours
6. Turn-over and cook for 30 minutes more
7. Once the internal temperature reaches 165 degrees Fahrenheit
8. Remove from the smoker and cover with foil
9. Allow it to rest for 15 minutes
10. Enjoy!

Nutrition Info: Calories: 237 Fats: 6.1g Carbs: 14g Fiber: 3g

124.   Smoking Duck With Mandarin Glaze

Servings: 4
Cooking Time: 4 Hours
Ingredients:
- 1 quart buttermilk
- 1 (5-pound) whole duck
- ¾ cup soy sauce
- ½ cup hoisin sauce
- ½ cup rice wine vinegar
- 2 tablespoons sesame oil
- 1 tablespoon freshly ground black pepper
- 1 tablespoon minced garlic
- Mandarin Glaze, for drizzling

Directions:
1.   With a very sharp knife, remove as much fat from the duck as you can. Refrigerate or freeze the fat for later use.
2.   Pour the buttermilk into a large container with a lid and submerge the whole duck in it. Cover and let brine in the refrigerator for 4 to 6 hours.
3.   Supply your smoker with wood pellets and follow the manufacturer's specific start-up procedure. Preheat, with the lid closed, to 250°F.
4.   Remove the duck from the buttermilk brine, then rinse it and pat dry with paper towels.
5.   In a bowl, combine the soy sauce, hoisin sauce, vinegar, sesame oil, pepper, and garlic to form a paste. Reserve ¼ cup for basting.
6.   Poke holes in the skin of the duck and rub the remaining paste all over and inside the cavity.
7.   Place the duck on the grill breast-side down, close the lid, and smoke for about 4 hours, basting every hour with the reserved paste, until a meat thermometer inserted in the thickest part of the meat reads 165°F. Use aluminum foil to tent the duck in the last 30 minutes or so if it starts to brown too quickly.
8.   To finish, drizzle with glaze.

125.   Easy Rapid-fire Roast Chicken

Servings: 4
Cooking Time: 1 To 2 Hours
Ingredients:
- 1 (4-pound) whole chicken, giblets removed
- Extra-virgin olive oil, for rubbing
- 3 tablespoons Greek seasoning
- Juice of 1 lemon
- Butcher's string

Directions:
1.   Supply your smoker with wood pellets and follow the manufacturer's specific start-up procedure. Preheat, with the lid closed, to 450°F.
2.   Rub the bird generously all over with oil, including inside the cavity.
3.   Sprinkle the Greek seasoning all over and under the skin of the bird, and squeeze the lemon juice over the breast.
4.   Tuck the chicken wings behind the back and tie the legs together with butcher's string or cooking twine.
5.   Put the chicken directly on the grill, breast-side up, close the lid, and roast for 1 hour to 1 hour 30 minutes, or until a meat thermometer inserted in the thigh reads 165°F.
6.   Let the meat rest for 10 minutes before carving.

126.   Perfectly Smoked Turkey Legs

Servings: 6
Cooking Time: 4 Hours
Ingredients:
- For Turkey:
- 3 tbsp. Worcestershire sauce
- 1 tbsp. canola oil
- 6 turkey legs
- For Rub:
- ¼ C. chipotle seasoning
- 1 tbsp. brown sugar
- 1 tbsp. paprika
- For Sauce:
- 1 C. white vinegar
- 1 tbsp. canola oil
- 1 tbsp. chipotle BBQ sauce

Directions:
1. For turkey in a bowl, add the Worcestershire sauce and canola oil and mix well.
2. With your fingers, loosen the skin of legs.
3. With your fingers coat the legs under the skin with oil mixture.
4. In another bowl, mix together rub ingredients.
5. Rub the spice mixture under and outer surface of turkey legs generously.
6. Transfer the legs into a large sealable bag and refrigerate for about 2-4 hours.
7. Remove the turkey legs from refrigerator and set aside at room temperature for at least 30 minutes before cooking.
8. Set the temperature of Grill to 200-220 degrees F and preheat with closed lid for 15 minutes.
9. In a small pan, mix together all sauce ingredients on low heat and cook until warmed completely, stirring continuously.
10. Place the turkey legs onto the grill cook for about 3½-4 hours, coating with sauce after every 45 minutes.
11. Serve hot.
Nutrition Info: Calories per serving: 430; Carbohydrates: 4.9g; Protein: 51.2g; Fat: 19.5g; Sugar: 3.9g; Sodium: 1474mg; Fiber: 0.5g

127.   Easy Smoked Chicken Breasts

Servings: 4
Cooking Time: 30 Minutes
Ingredients:
- 4 large chicken breasts, bones and skin removed
- 1 tablespoon olive oil
- 2 tablespoons brown sugar
- 2 tablespoons maple syrup
- 1 teaspoon celery seeds
- 2 tablespoons paprika
- 2 tablespoons salt
- 1 teaspoon black pepper
- 2 tablespoons garlic powder
- 2 tablespoons onion powder

Directions:
1. Place all ingredients in a bowl and massage the chicken with your hands. Place in the fridge to marinate for at least 4 hours.
2. Fire the Grill to 350F and use maple wood pellets. Close the lid and allow to preheat to 15 minutes.
3. Place the chicken on the grill a and cook for 15 minutes with the lid closed.
4. Turn the chicken over and cook for another 10 minutes.
5. Insert a thermometer into the thickest part of the chicken and make sure that the temperature reads to 165F.
6. Remove the chicken from the grill and allow to rest for 5 minutes before slicing.
Nutrition Info: Calories per serving: 327 ; Protein: 40 g; Carbs: 23g; Fat: 9g Sugar: 13g

128.   Roasted Whole Chicken

Servings: 6 To 8
Cooking Time: 1 To 2 Hours
Ingredients:
- 1 whole chicken
- 2 tablespoons olive oil
- 1 batch Chicken Rub

Directions:
1. Supply your smoker with wood pellets and follow the manufacturer's specific start-up procedure. Preheat the grill, with the lid closed, to 375°F.
2. Coat the chicken all over with olive oil and season it with the rub. Using your hands, work the rub into the meat.
3. Place the chicken directly on the grill grate and smoke until its internal temperature reaches 170°F.
4. Remove the chicken from the grill and let it rest for 10 minutes, before carving and serving.

129.   Game Day Chicken Drumsticks

Servings: 8
Cooking Time: 1 Hour
Ingredients:
- For Brine:
- ½ C. brown sugar
- ½ C. kosher salt
- 5 C. water
- 2 (12-oz.) bottles beer
- 8 chicken drumsticks
- For Coating:
- ¼ C. olive oil
- ½ C. BBQ rub
- 1 tbsp. fresh parsley, minced
- 1 tbsp. fresh chives, minced
- ¾ C. BBQ sauce
- ¼ C. beer

Directions:
1. For brine: in a bucket, dissolve brown sugar and kosher salt in water and beer.
2. Place the chicken drumsticks in brine and refrigerate, covered for about 3 hours.
3. Set the temperature of Grill to 275 degrees F and preheat with closed lid for 15 minutes.
4. Remove chicken drumsticks from brine and rinse under cold running water.
5. With paper towels, pat dry chicken drumsticks.
6. Coat drumsticks with olive oil and rub with BBQ rub evenly.
7. Sprinkle the drumsticks with parsley and chives.
8. Arrange the chicken drumsticks onto the grill and cook for about 45 minutes.
9. Meanwhile, in a bowl, mix together BBQ sauce and beer.
10. Remove from grill and coat the drumsticks with BBQ sauce evenly.
11. Cook for about 15 minutes more.
12. Serve immediately.

Nutrition Info: Calories per serving: 448; Carbohydrates: 20.5g; Protein: 47.2g; Fat: 16.1g; Sugar: 14.9g; Sodium: 9700mg; Fiber: 0.2g

130. Jamaican Jerk Chicken Quarters

Servings: 4
Cooking Time: 1 To 2 Hours

Ingredients:

- 4 chicken leg quarters, scored
- ¼ cup canola oil
- ½ cup Jamaican Jerk Paste
- 1 tablespoon whole allspice (pimento) berries

Directions:

1. Supply your smoker with wood pellets and follow the manufacturer's specific start-up procedure. Preheat, with the lid closed, to 275°F.
2. Brush the chicken with canola oil, then brush 6 tablespoons of the Jerk paste on and under the skin. Reserve the remaining 2 tablespoons of paste for basting.
3. Throw the whole allspice berries in with the wood pellets for added smoke flavor.
4. Arrange the chicken on the grill, close the lid, and smoke for 1 hour to 1 hour 30 minutes, or until a meat thermometer inserted in the thickest part of the thigh reads 165°F.
5. Let the meat rest for 5 minutes and baste with the reserved jerk paste prior to serving.

BEEF, PORK & LAMB RECIPES

131.   Maple-smoked Pork Chops

Servings: 4
Cooking Time: 55 Minutes
Ingredients:
- 1 (12-pound) full packer brisket
- 2 tablespoons yellow mustard
- 1 batch Espresso Brisket Rub
- Worcestershire Mop and Spritz, for spritzing

Directions:
1. Supply your smoker with wood pellets and follow the manufacturer's specific start-up procedure. Preheat the grill, with the lid closed, to 180°F.
2. Season the pork chops on both sides with salt and pepper.
3. Place the chops directly on the grill grate and smoke for 30 minutes.
4. Increase the grill's temperature to 350°F. Continue to cook the chops until their internal temperature reaches 145°F.
5. Remove the pork chops from the grill and let them rest for 5 minutes before serving.

132.   Braised Pork Chile Verde

Servings: 6
Cooking Time: 40 Minutes
Ingredients:
- 3 pounds pork shoulder, bone removed and cut into ½ inch cubes
- 1 tablespoon all-purpose flour
- Salt and pepper to taste
- 1-pound tomatillos, husked and washed
- 2 jalapenos, chopped
- 1 medium yellow onion, peeled and cut into chunks
- 4 cloves of garlic
- 4 tablespoons extra virgin olive oil
- 2 cup chicken stock
- 2 cans green chilies
- 1 tablespoon cumin
- 1 tablespoon oregano
- ½ lime, juiced
- ¼ cup cilantro

Directions:
1. Place the pork shoulder chunks in a bowl and toss with flour. Season with salt and pepper to taste.
2. When ready to cook, fire the Grill to 500F. Use desired wood pellets when cooking. Place a large cast iron skillet on the bottom rack of the grill. Close the lid and preheat for 15 minutes.
3. Place the tomatillos, jalapeno, onion, and garlic on a sheet tray lined with foil and drizzle with 2 tablespoon olive oil. Season with salt and pepper to taste.
4. Place the remaining olive oil in the heated cast iron skillet and cook the pork shoulder. Spread the meat evenly then close.
5. Before closing the lid, place the vegetables in the tray on the grill rack. Close the lid of the grill.
6. Cook for 20 minutes without opening the lid or stirring the pork. After 20 minutes, remove the vegetables from the grill and transfer to a blender. Pulse until smooth and pour into the pan with the pork.
7. Stir in the chicken stock, green chilies, cumin, oregano, and lime juice. Season with salt and pepper to taste.
8. Close the grill lid and cook for another 20 minutes.
9. Once cooked, stir in the cilantro.
Nutrition Info: Calories per serving: 389; Protein: 28.5g; Carbs: 4.5g; Fat: 24.3g Sugar: 2.1g

133. Bacon

Servings: 6
Cooking Time: 25 Minutes
Ingredients:
- 1lb bacon

Directions:
1. Preheat your to 375F.
2. Line a baking sheet with parchment paper then arrange the thick-cut bacon on it in a single layer.
3. Bake the bacon in the for 20 minutes. Flip the bacon pieces and cook for 20 more minutes or until the bacon is no longer floppy.
4. Serve and enjoy.

Nutrition Info: Calories 315, Total fat 10g, Saturated fat 0g, Total carbs 0g, Net carbs 0g Protein 9g, Sugars 0g, Fiber 0g, Sodium 500mg

134. Boneless Leg Of Lamb

Servings: 4
Cooking Time: 4 Hours
Ingredients:
- 2 1/2 pounds leg of lamb, boneless, fat trimmed
- For the Marinade:
- 2 teaspoons minced garlic
- 1 tablespoon ground black pepper
- 2 tablespoons salt
- 1 teaspoon thyme
- 2 tablespoons oregano
- 2 tablespoons olive oil

Directions:
1. Take a small bowl, place all the ingredients for the marinade in it and then stir until combined.
2. Rub the marinade on all sides of lamb, then place it in a large sheet, cover with a plastic wrap and marinate for a minimum of 1 hour in the refrigerator.
3. When ready to cook, switch on the grill, fill the grill hopper with apple-flavored wood pellets, power the grill on by using the control panel, select 'smoke' on the temperature dial, or set the temperature to 250 degrees F and let it preheat for a minimum of 5 minutes.
4. Meanwhile,
5. When the grill has preheated, open the lid, place the lamb on the grill grate, shut the grill and smoke for 4 hours until the internal temperature reaches 145 degrees F.
6. When done, transfer lamb to a cutting board, let it stand for 10 minutes, then carve it into slices and serve.

Nutrition Info: Calories: 213 Cal ;Fat: 9 g ;Carbs: 1 g ;Protein: 29 g ;Fiber: 0 g

135.   Roasted Whole Ham In Apricot Sauce

Servings: 12
Cooking Time: 2 Hours
Ingredients:
- 8-pound whole ham, bone-in
- 16 ounces apricot BBQ sauce
- 2 tablespoon Dijon mustard
- 1/4 cup horseradish

Directions:
1.   Switch on the grill, fill the grill hopper with apple-flavored wood pellets, power the grill on by using the control panel, select 'smoke' on the temperature dial, or set the temperature to 325 degrees F and let it preheat for a minimum of 15 minutes.
2.   Meanwhile, take a large roasting pan, line it with foil, and place ham on it.
3.   When the grill has preheated, open the lid, place roasting pan containing ham on the grill grate, shut the grill and smoke for 1 hour and 30 minutes.
4.   Meanwhile, prepare the glaze and for this, take a medium saucepan, place it over medium heat, add BBQ sauce, mustard, and horseradish, stir until mixed and cook for 5 minutes, set aside until required.
5.   After 1 hour and 30 minutes smoking, brush ha generously with the prepared glaze and continue smoking for 30 minutes until internal temperature reaches 135 degrees F.
6.   When done, remove roasting pan from the grill, let rest for 20 minutes and then cut into slices. Serve ham with remaining glaze.
Nutrition Info: Calories: 157.7 Cal ;Fat: 5.6 g ;Carbs: 4.1 g ;Protein: 22.1 g ;Fiber: 0.1 g

136.   Fall-of-the-bones Short Ribs

Servings: 4
Cooking Time: 5½ Hours
Ingredients:
- 2½ lb. beef short ribs, trimmed
- 4 tbsp. extra-virgin olive oil
- 4 tbsp. beef rub
- 1 C. apple juice
- 1 C. apple cider vinegar
- 1 C. red wine
- 1 C. beef broth
- 2 tbsp. butter
- 2 tbsp. Worcestershire sauce
- Salt and freshly ground black pepper, to taste

Directions:
1.   Set the temperature of Grill to 225 degrees F and preheat with closed lid for 15 minutes.
2.   Coat the ribs with olive oil and season with rub evenly.
3.   Arrange the ribs onto the grill and cook for about 1 hour.
4.   In a food-safe spray bottle, mix together apple juice and vinegar.
5.   After 1 hour spray the ribs with vinegar mixture evenly.
6.   Cook for about 2 hours, spraying with vinegar mixture after every 15 minutes.
7.   In a bowl, mix together remaining ingredients.
8.   Transfer the ribs in a baking dish with wine mixture.
9.   With a piece of foil, cover the baking dish tightly and cook for about 2-2½ hours.
10.   Remove the ribs from grill and place onto a cutting board for about 10-15 minutes before slicing.
11.   With a sharp knife, cut the ribs into equal-sized individual ribs and serve.
Nutrition Info: Calories per serving: 859; Carbohydrates: 10.9g; Protein: 83.2g; Fat: 45.7g; Sugar: 8.4g; Sodium: 532mg; Fiber: 0.1g

137.   St. Louis Bbq Ribs

Servings: 4-6
Cooking Time: 4 Hours 20 Minutes
Ingredients:
- pork as well as a poultry rub - 6 oz
- St. Louis bone in the form of pork ribs - 2 racks
- Heat and Sweet BBQ sauce - 1 bottle
- Apple juice - 8 oz

Directions:
1.   Trim the ribs and peel off their membranes from the back.
2.   Apply an even coat of the poultry rub on the front and back of the ribs. Let the coat sit for at least 20 minutes. If you wish to refrigerate it, you can do so for up to 4 hours.
3.   Once you are ready to cook it, preheat the pellet grill for around 15 minutes. Place the ribs on the grill grate, bone side down. Put the apple juice in an easy spray bottle and then spray it evenly on the ribs.
4.   Smoke the meat for 1 hour.
5.   Remove the ribs from the pellet grill and wrap them securely in aluminum foil. Ensure that there is an opening in the wrapping at one end. Pour the remaining 6 oz of apple juice into the foil. Wrap it tightly.
6.   Place the ribs on the grill again, meat side down. Smoke the meat for another 3 hours.
7.   Once the ribs are done and cooked evenly, get rid of the foil. Gently brush a layer of the sauce on both sides of the ribs. Put them back on the grill to cook for another 10 minutes to ensure that the sauce is set correctly.
8.   Once the sauce sets, take the ribs off the pellet grill and rest for at least 10 minutes to soak in all the juices.
9.   Slice the ribs to serve and enjoy!
Nutrition Info: Carbohydrates: 13 g Protein: 67 g Fat: 70 g Sodium: 410 mg Cholesterol: 180 mg

138.   Simply Delicious Tri Tip Roast

Servings: 8
Cooking Time: 35 Minutes
Ingredients:
- 1 tbsp. granulated onion
- 1 tbsp. granulated garlic
- Salt and freshly ground black pepper, to taste
- 1 (3-lb.) tri tip roast, trimmed

Directions:
1.   In a bowl, add all ingredients except for roast and mix well.
2.   Coat the roast with spice mixture generously.
3.   Set aside at room temperature until grill heats.
4.   Set the temperature of Grill to 250 degrees F and preheat with closed lid for 15 minutes.
5.   Place the roast onto the grill and cook for about 25 minutes.
6.   Now, set the grill to 350-400 degrees F and preheat with closed lid for 15 minutes. and sear roast for about 3-5 minutes per side.
7.   Remove the roast from grill and place onto a cutting board for about 15-20 minutes before slicing.
8.   With a sharp knife, cut the roast into slices across the grain and serve.
Nutrition Info: Calories per serving: 313; Carbohydrates: 0.8g; Protein: 45.7g; Fat: 14.2g; Sugar: 0.3g; Sodium: 115mg; Fiber: 0.1g

139.   Simple Grilled Lamb Chops

Servings: 6
Cooking Time: 6 Minutes
Ingredients:
- 1/4 cup distilled white vinegar
- 2 tbsp salt
- 1/2 tbsp black pepper
- 1 tbsp garlic, minced
- 1 onion, thinly sliced
- 2 tbsp olive oil
- 2lb lamb chops

Directions:
1. In a resealable bag, mix vinegar, salt, black pepper, garlic, sliced onion, and oil until all salt has dissolved.
2. Add the lamb chops and toss until well coated. Place in the fridge to marinate for 2 hours.
3. Preheat the wood pellet grill to high heat.
4. Remove the lamb from the fridge and discard the marinade. Wrap any exposed bones with foil.
5. Grill the lamb for 3 minutes per side. You can also broil in a broiler for more crispness.
6. Serve and enjoy

Nutrition Info: Calories 519, Total fat 44.8g, Saturated fat 18g, Total Carbs 2.3g, Net Carbs 1.9g, Protein 25g, Sugar1g, Fiber 0.4g, Sodium: 861mg, Potassium 359mg

140.   Thai Beef Skewers

Servings: 6
Cooking Time: 8 Minutes
Ingredients:
- ½ of medium red bell pepper, destemmed, cored, cut into a ¼-inch piece
- ½ of beef sirloin, fat trimmed
- ½ cup salted peanuts, roasted, chopped
- For the Marinade:
- 1 teaspoon minced garlic
- 1 tablespoon grated ginger
- 1 lime, juiced
- 1 teaspoon ground black pepper
- 1 tablespoon sugar
- 1/4 cup soy sauce
- 1/4 cup olive oil

Directions:
1. Prepare the marinade and for this, take a small bowl, place all of its ingredients in it, whisk until combined, and then pour it into a large plastic bag.
2. Cut into beef sirloin 1-1/4-inch dice, add to the plastic bag containing marinade, seal the bag, turn it upside down to coat beef pieces with the marinade and let it marinate for a minimum of 2 hours in the refrigerator.
3. When ready to cook, switch on the grill, fill the grill hopper with cherry flavored wood pellets, power the grill on by using the control panel, select 'smoke' on the temperature dial, or set the temperature to 425 degrees F and let it preheat for a minimum of 5 minutes.
4. Meanwhile, remove beef pieces from the marinade and then thread onto skewers.
5. When the grill has preheated, open the lid, place prepared skewers on the grill grate, shut the grill, and smoke for 4 minutes per side until done.
6. When done, transfer skewers to a dish, sprinkle with peanuts and red pepper, and then serve.

Nutrition Info: Calories: 124 Cal ;Fat: 5.5 g ;Carbs: 1.7 g ;Protein: 15.6 g ;Fiber: 0 g

141.   Garlic And Rosemary Grilled Lamb Chops

Servings: 4
Cooking Time: 20 Minutes
Ingredients:
- 2 lb lamb loin, thick-cut
- 4 garlic cloves, minced
- 1 tbsp kosher salt
- 1/2 tbsp black pepper
- 1 lemon zest
- 1/4 cup olive oil

Directions:
1.   In a small mixing bowl, mix garlic, lemon zest, oil, salt, and black pepper then pour the mixture over the lamb.
2.   Flip the lamb chops to make sure they are evenly coated. Place the chops in the fridge to marinate for an hour.
3.   Preheat the wood pellet grill to high heat then sear the lamb for 3 minutes on each side.
4.   Reduce the heat and cook the chops for 6 minutes or until the internal temperature reaches 150 F.
5.   Remove the lamb from the grill and wrap it in a foil. Let it rest for 5 minutes before serving. Enjoy.
Nutrition Info: Calories 171.5, Total fat 7.8g, Saturated fat 2.5g, Total Carbs 0.4g, Net Carbs 0.3g, Protein 23.2g, Sugar 0g, Fiber 0.1g, Sodium: 72.8mg, Potassium 393.8mg

142.   Naked St. Louis Ribs

Servings: 6-8
Cooking Time: 5-6 Hours
Ingredients:
- 3 St. Louis-style pork blacks
- 1 cup and 1 tablespoon of Yang's original dry lab or your favorite pork club

Directions:
1.   Insert the spoon handle between the membrane and the rib bone and remove the membrane under the rib bone rack. Grasp the membrane with a paper towel and pull it down slowly from the rack to remove it.
2.   Rub both sides of the rib with a sufficient amount of friction.
3.   Use of wood pellet smokers and grills
4.   Configure a wood pellet smoker grill for indirect cooking and preheat to 225 ° F using hickory or apple pellets.
5.   If using Reblack, place the ribs on the grill grid rack. Otherwise, you can use a Teflon-coated fiberglass mat or place the ribs directly on the grill.
6.   Slice rib bone at 225 ° F for 5-6 hours with hickory pellets until the internal temperature of the thickest part of the ick bone reaches 185 ° F to 190 ° F.
7.   Place ribs under loose foil tent for 10 minutes before carving and serving.
Nutrition Info: Calories: 320 Cal Fat: 26 g Carbohydrates: 0 g   Protein: 19 g Fiber: 0 g

143.   Mesquite Smoked Brisket

Servings: 8 To 12
Cooking Time: 12 To 16 Hours
Ingredients:
- 1 (12-pound) full packer brisket
- 2 tablespoons yellow mustard (you can also use soy sauce)
- Salt
- Freshly ground black pepper

Directions:
1. Supply your with wood pellets and follow the start-up procedure. Preheat the grill, with the lid closed, to 225°F.
2. Using a boning knife, carefully remove all but about ½ inch of the large layer of fat covering one side of your brisket.
3. Coat the brisket all over with mustard and season it with salt and pepper.
4. Place the brisket directly on the grill grate and smoke until its internal temperature reaches 160°F and the brisket has formed a dark bark.
5. Pull the brisket from the grill and wrap it completely in aluminum foil or butcher paper.
6. Increase the grill's temperature to 350°F and return the wrapped brisket to it. Continue to cook until its internal temperature reaches 190°F.
7. Transfer the wrapped brisket to a cooler, cover the cooler, and let the brisket rest for 1 or 2 hours.
8. Remove the brisket from the cooler and unwrap it.
9. Separate the brisket point from the flat by cutting along the fat layer, and slice the flat. The point can be saved for burnt ends (see Sweet Heat Burnt Ends), or sliced and served as well.

144.   Pork Belly

Servings: 8
Cooking Time: 3 Hours And 30 Minutes
Ingredients:
- 3 pounds pork belly, skin removed
- Pork and poultry rub as needed
- 4 tablespoons salt
- 1/2 teaspoon ground black pepper

Directions:
1. Switch on the grill, fill the grill hopper with apple-flavored wood pellets, power the grill on by using the control panel, select 'smoke' on the temperature dial, or set the temperature to 275 degrees F and let it preheat for a minimum of 15 minutes.
2. Meanwhile, prepare the pork belly and for this, sprinkle pork and poultry rub, salt, and black pepper on all sides of pork belly until well coated.
3. When the grill has preheated, open the lid, place the pork belly on the grill grate, shut the grill and smoke for 3 hours and 30 minutes until the internal temperature reaches 200 degrees F.
4. When done, transfer pork belly to a cutting board, let it rest for 15 minutes, then cut it into slices and serve.

Nutrition Info: Calories: 430 Cal ;Fat: 44 g ;Carbs: 1 g ;Protein: 8 g ;Fiber: 0 g

145.   Smoked Pulled Pork

Servings: 4
Cooking Time: 6 Hours
Ingredients:
- 2 pounds bone-in pork shoulder
- Big Game Rub
- 2 cups apple cider
- 'Que BBQ Sauce

Directions:
1.   Place the pork shoulder in a bowl and remove excess fat and season with the Big Game Rub.
2.   When ready to cook, fire the Grill to 250F. Use maple wood pellets when cooking. Close the lid and preheat for 15 minutes.
3.   Place pork on the grill grate for 5 hours or until the internal temperature reaches 160F.
4.   Remove the pork from the grill and allow to rest.
5.   On a baking sheet, stack 4 pieces of aluminum foil on top of each other. Place the pork in the center of the foil and bring up the sides of the foil to create a sleeve around the pork. Scrimp the edges to ensure that any liquid does not escape from the sleeve. Pour over the apple cider.
6.   Place the foil-wrapped pork on the grill and cook for another 3 hours at 2040F.
7.   Remove from the grill and allow to rest.
8.   Remove the pork from the foil sleeve and transfer to a plate, use forks to shred the meat. Discard the bones if any.
9.   Once the pork has been shredded pour over the BBQ sauce.
Nutrition Info: Calories per serving: 634; Protein: 57g; Carbs: 7.6g; Fat: 40.2g Sugar: 5.7g

146.   Smoked Pork Sausages

Servings: 6
Cooking Time: 1 Hour
Ingredients:
- 3 pounds ground pork
- ½ tablespoon ground mustard
- 1 tablespoon onion powder
- 1 tablespoon garlic powder
- 1 teaspoon pink curing salt
- 1 teaspoon salt
- 1 teaspoon black pepper
- ¼ cup ice water
- Hog casings, soaked and rinsed in cold water

Directions:
1.   Mix all ingredients except for the hog casings in a bowl. Using your hands, mix until all ingredients are well-combined.
2.   Using a sausage stuffer, stuff the hog casings with the pork mixture.
3.   Measure 4 inches of the stuffed hog casing and twist to form into a sausage. Repeat the process until you create sausage links.
4.   When ready to cook, fire the Grill to 225F. Use apple wood pellets when cooking the ribs. Close the lid and preheat for 15 minutes.
5.   Place the sausage links on the grill grate and cook for 1 hour or until the internal temperature of the sausage reads at 155F.
6.   Allow to rest before slicing.
Nutrition Info: Calories per serving: 688; Protein: 58.9g; Carbs: 2.7g; Fat: 47.3g Sugar: 0.2g

147.   Tender Flank Steak

Servings: 6
Cooking Time: 10 Minutes
Ingredients:
- ½ C. olive oil
- 1/3 C. fresh lemon juice
- 1/3 C. soy sauce
- ¼ C. brown sugar
- 2 tbsp. Worcestershire sauce
- 5 garlic cloves, minced
- 1 tsp. red chili powder
- 1 tsp. red pepper flakes, crushed
- 2 lb. flank steak

Directions:
1. In a resealable plastic bag, add all ingredients except for steak and mix well.
2. Place the steak and seal the bag.
3. Shake the bag vigorously to coat well.
4. Refrigerate to marinate overnight.
5. Set the temperature of Grill to 450 degrees F and preheat with closed lid for 15 minutes.
6. Place the steak onto the grill and cook for about 5 minutes per side.
7. Remove the steak from grill and place onto a cutting board for about 10 minutes before slicing.
8. With a sharp knife, cut the steak into slices across the grain.

Nutrition Info: Calories per serving: 482; Carbohydrates: 9.5g; Protein: 43.3g; Fat: 29.6g; Sugar: 7.5g; Sodium: 948mg; Fiber: 0.4g

148.   Pulled Beef

Servings: 5 To 8
Cooking Time: 12 To 14 Hours
Ingredients:
- 1 (4-pound) top round roast
- 2 tablespoons yellow mustard
- 1 batch Espresso Brisket Rub
- ½ cup beef broth

Directions:
1. Supply your with wood pellets and follow the start-up procedure. Preheat the grill, with the lid closed, to 225°F.
2. Coat the top round roast all over with mustard and season it with the rub. Using your hands, work the rub into the meat.
3. Place the roast directly on the grill grate and smoke until its internal temperature reaches 160°F and a dark bark has formed.
4. Pull the roast from the grill and place it on enough aluminum foil to wrap it completely.
5. Increase the grill's temperature to 350°F.
6. Fold in three sides of the foil around the roast and add the beef broth. Fold in the last side, completely enclosing the roast and liquid. Return the wrapped roast to the grill and cook until its internal temperature reaches 195°F.
7. Pull the roast from the grill and place it in a cooler. Cover the cooler and let the roast rest for 1 or 2 hours.
8. Remove the roast from the cooler and unwrap it. Pull apart the beef using just your fingers. Serve immediately.

149.   Citrus-brined Pork Roast

Servings: 6
Cooking Time: 45 Minutes
Ingredients:
- ½ cup salt
- ¼ cup brown sugar
- 3 cloves of garlic, minced
- 2 dried bay leaves
- 6 peppercorns
- 1 lemon, juiced
- ½ teaspoon dried fennel seeds
- ½ teaspoon red pepper flakes
- ½ cup apple juice
- ½ cup orange juice
- 5 pounds pork loin
- 2 tablespoons extra virgin olive oil

Directions:
1.   In a bowl, combine the salt, brown sugar, garlic, bay leaves, peppercorns, lemon juice, fennel seeds, pepper flakes, apple juice, and orange juice. Mix to form a paste rub.
2.   Rub the mixture on to the pork loin and allow to marinate for at least 2 hours in the fridge. Add in the oil.
3.   When ready to cook, fire the Grill to 300F. Use apple wood pellets when cooking. Close the lid and preheat for 15 minutes.
4.   Place the seasoned pork loin on the grill grate and close the lid. Cook for 45 minutes. Make sure to flip the pork halfway through the cooking time.

Nutrition Info: Calories per serving: 869; Protein: 97.2g; Carbs: 15.2g; Fat: 43.9g Sugar: 13g

150.   Smoked Pork Ribs

Servings: 4
Cooking Time: 10 Hours
Ingredients:
- 2 racks back ribs
- 1 cup homemade bbq rub
- 2 12-oz hard apple cider
- 1 cup dark brown sugar
- 2 batches homemade BBQ sauce

Directions:
1.   Turn the to smoke setting and remove any membrane from the meat.
2.   Place the pork in the and smoke for 5 hours or until it reaches an internal temperature of 175.
3.   Increase the grill temperature to 225F. Transfer the meat to a pan sprayed with cooking spray.
4.   Pour one bottle of hard apple cider to the pan and rub the brown sugar on top of the ribs.
5.   Cover the pan with tin foil and place it back to the Traeger. Cook for 4 hours.
6.   Remove the tin foil, increase the temperature to 300F, and place the ribs on the grill grates.
7.   Cook for 1 hour brushing the ribs with BBQ sauce 3 times.
8.   The ribs should now be falling off the bone. Let rest for 5 minutes before serving.

Nutrition Info: Calories 1073, Total fat 42g, Saturated fat 15g, Total carbs 111g, Net carbs 109g Protein 61g, Sugars 99g, Fiber 3g, Sodium 1663mg

151.   Smoked Longhorn Cowboy Tri-tip

Servings: 7
Cooking Time: 4 Hours
Ingredients:
- 3 lb tri-tip roast
- 1/8 cup coffee, ground
- 1/4 cup beef rub

Directions:
1. Preheat the grill to 180°F with the lid closed for 15 minutes.
2. Meanwhile, rub the roast with coffee and beef rub. Place the roast on the grill grate and smoke for 3 hours.
3. Remove the roast from the grill and double wrap it with foil. Increase the temperature to 275°F.
4. Return the meat to the grill and let cook for 90 minutes or until the internal temperature reaches 135°F.
5. Remove from the grill, unwrap it and let rest for 10 minutes before serving.
6. Enjoy.

Nutrition Info: Calories 245, Total fat 14g, Saturated fat 4g, Total Carbs 0g, Net Carbs 0g, Protein 23g, Sugar 0g, Fiber 0g, Sodium: 80mg

152.   Foolproof Lamb Chops

Servings: 4
Cooking Time: 17 Minutes
Ingredients:
- ½ C. extra-virgin olive oil, divided
- ¼ C. onion, chopped roughly
- 2 garlic cloves, chopped roughly
- 2 tbsp. balsamic vinegar
- 2 tbsp. soy sauce
- 1 tsp. Worcestershire sauce
- 1 tbsp. fresh rosemary, chopped
- 2 tsp. Dijon mustard
- Freshly ground black pepper, to taste
- 4 (5-oz.) lamb chops
- Salt, to taste

Directions:
1. In a small pan, heat 1 tbsp. of olive oil over medium heat and sauté the onion and garlic for about 4-5 minutes.
2. Remove from the heat and transfer into a blender.
3. In the blender, add the vinegar, soy sauce, Worcestershire sauce, rosemary, mustard and black pepper and pulse until well combined.
4. While the motor is running, slowly add the remaining oil and pulse until smooth.
5. Transfer the sauce into a bowl and set aside.
6. Set the temperature of Grill to 500 degrees F and preheat with closed lid for 15 minutes.
7. Coat the lamb chops with remaining oil and then, season with salt and black pepper evenly.
8. Arrange the chops onto the grill and cook for about 4-6 minutes per side.
9. Remove the chops from grill and serve hot alongside the sauce.

Nutrition Info: Calories per serving: 496; Carbohydrates: 2.8g; Protein: 40.6g; Fat: 35.8g; Sugar: 0.8g; Sodium: 641mg; Fiber: 0.7g

153.   Smoked Lamb Meatballs

Servings: 20
Cooking Time: 1 Hour
Ingredients:
- 1 lb. lamb shoulder, ground
- 3 garlic cloves, finely diced
- 3 tbsp. shallot, diced
- 1 tbsp. salt
- 1 egg
- 1/2 tbsp. pepper
- 1/2 tbsp. cumin
- 1/2 tbsp. smoked paprika
- 1/4 tbsp. red pepper flakes
- 1/4 tbsp. cinnamon
- 1/4 cup panko breadcrumbs

Directions:
1. Set your to 250F .
2. Combine all the ingredients in a small bowl then mix thoroughly using your hands.
3. Form golf ball-sized meatballs and place them in a baking sheet.
4. Place the baking sheet in the smoker and smoke until the internal temperature reaches 160F.
5. Remove the meatballs from the smoker and serve when hot.

Nutrition Info: Calories 93, Total fat 5.9g, Saturated fat 2.5g, Total carbs 4.8g, Net carbs 4.5g Protein 5g, Sugars 0.3g, Fiber 0.3g, Sodium 174.1mg, Potassium 82.8mg

154.   Wine Braised Lamb Shank

Servings: 2
Cooking Time: 10 Hours
Ingredients:
- 2 (1¼-lb.) lamb shanks
- 1-2 C. water
- ¼ C. brown sugar
- 1/3 C. rice wine
- 1/3 C. soy sauce
- 1 tbsp. dark sesame oil
- 4 (1½x½-inch) orange zest strips
- 2 (3-inch long) cinnamon sticks
- 1½ tsp. Chinese five-spice powder

Directions:
1. Set the temperature of Grill to 225-250 degrees F and preheat with closed lid for 15 minutes. , using charcoal and soaked apple wood chips.
2. With a sharp knife, pierce each lamb shank at many places.
3. In a bowl, add remaining all ingredients and mix until sugar is dissolved.
4. In a large foil pan, place the lamb shanks and top with sugar mixture evenly.
5. Place the foil pan onto the grill and cook for about 8-10 hours, flipping after every 30 minutes. (If required, add enough water to keep the liquid ½-inch over).
6. Remove from the grill and serve hot.

Nutrition Info: Calories per serving: 1200; Carbohydrates: 39.7g; Protein: 161.9g; Fat: 48.4; Sugar: 29g; Sodium: 2000mg; Fiber: 0.3g

155. Wood Pellet Grilled Lamb With Brown Sugar Glaze

Servings: 4
Cooking Time: 10 Minutes
Ingredients:
- 1/4 cup brown sugar
- 2 tbsp ginger, ground
- 2 tbsp tarragon, dried
- 1 tbs cinnamon, ground
- 1 tbsp black pepper, ground
- 1 tbsp garlic powder
- 1/2 tbsp salt
- 4 lamb chops

Directions:
1. In a mixing bowl, mix sugar, ginger, dried tarragon, cinnamon, black pepper, garlic, and salt.
2. Rub the lamb chops with the seasoning and place it on a plate.refrigerate for an hour to marinate.
3. Preheat the grill to high heat then brush the grill grate with oil.
4. Arrange the lamb chops on the grill grate in a single layer and cook for 5 minutes on each side.
5. Serve and enjoy.

Nutrition Info: Calories 241, Total fat 13.1g, Saturated fat 6g, Total Carbs 15.8g, Net Carbs 15.1g, Protein 14.6g, Sugar 14g, Fiber 0.7g, Sodium: 339mg,

156. New York Strip

Servings: 6
Cooking Time: 15 Minutes
Ingredients:
- 3 New York strips
- Salt and pepper

Directions:
1. If the steak is in the fridge, remove it 30 minutes prior to cooking.
2. Preheat the
3. to 450F.
4. Meanwhile, season the steak generously with salt and pepper. Place it on the grill and let it cook for 5 minutes per side or until the internal temperature reaches 1280F.
5. Rest for 10 minutes.

Nutrition Info: Calories: 198 Cal Fat: 14 g Carbohydrates: 0 g Protein: 17 g Fiber: 0 g

157. Lamb Shank

Servings: 6
Cooking Time: 4 Hours
Ingredients:
- 8-ounce red wine
- 2-ounce whiskey
- 2 tablespoons minced fresh rosemary
- 1 tablespoon minced garlic
- Black pepper
- 6 (1¼-pound) lamb shanks

Directions:
1. In a bowl, add all ingredients except lamb shank and mix till well combined.
2. In a large resealable bag, add marinade and lamb shank.
3. Seal the bag and shake to coat completely.
4. Refrigerate for about 24 hours.
5. Preheat the pallet grill to 225 degrees F.
6. Arrange the leg of lamb in pallet grill and cook for about 4 hours.

Nutrition Info: Calories: 1507 Cal Fat: 62 g Carbohydrates: 68.7 g Protein:163.3 g Fiber: 6 g

158.　Spicy Pork Chops

Servings: 4
Cooking Time: 10-15 Minutes
Ingredients:
- 1 tbsp. olive oil
- 2 cloves garlic, crushed and minced
- 1 tbsp. cayenne pepper
- ½ tsp. hot sauce
- ¼ cup lime juice
- 2 tsp. ground cumin
- 1 tsp. ground cinnamon
- 4 pork chops
- Lettuce

Directions:
1. Mix the olive oil, garlic, cayenne pepper, hot sauce, lime juice, cumin and cinnamon.
2. Pour the mixture into a re-sealable plastic bag. Place the pork chops inside. Seal and turn to coat evenly. Chill in the refrigerator for 4 hours. Grill for 10 to 15 minutes, flipping occasionally.
Nutrition Info: Calories: 196 Cal Fat: 9 g Carbohydrates: 3 g   Protein: 25 g Fiber: 1 g

159.　Apple-smoked Bacon

Servings: 4 To 6
Cooking Time: 20 To 30 Minutes
Ingredients:
- 1 (1-pound) package thick-sliced bacon

Directions:
1. Supply your smoker with wood pellets and follow the manufacturer's specific start-up procedure. Preheat the grill, with the lid closed, to 275°F.
2. Supply your smoker with wood pellets and follow the manufacturer's specific start-up procedure. Preheat the grill, with the lid closed, to 275°F.

160.　Reverse Seared Flank Steak

Servings: 2
Cooking Time: 20 Minutes
Ingredients:
- 3 pound flank steaks
- 1 tbsp salt
- 1/2 tbsp onion powder
- 1/4 tbsp garlic powder
- 1/2 black pepper, coarsely ground

Directions:
1. Preheat the to 225F.
2. Add the steaks and rub them generously with the rub mixture.
3. Place the steak
4. Let cook until its internal temperature is 100F under your desired temperature. 115F for rare, 125F for the medium rear and 135F for medium.
5. Wrap the steak with foil and raise the grill temperature to high. Place back the steak and grill for 3 minutes on each side.
6. Pat with butter and serve when hot.
Nutrition Info: Calories: 112 Cal Fat: 5 g Carbohydrates: 1 g   Protein: 16 g Fiber: 0 g

161.   Wood Pellet Smoked Spicy Candied Bacon

Servings: 6
Cooking Time: 35 Minutes
Ingredients:
- 1 lb centre cut bacon
- 1/2 cup dark brown sugar
- 1/2 cup maple syrup
- 1 tbsp sriracha hot sauce
- 1/2 tbsp cayenne pepper

Directions:
1. In a mixing bowl, combine sugar, maple syrup, sriracha sauce, and cayenne pepper.
2. Preheat the wood pellet grill to 300°F.
3. Line a baking pan with parchment paper and lay the bacon on it in a single layer. Brush the bacon with the sugar mixture until well coated.
4. Place the baking pan in the grill and cook for 20 minutes. Flip the bacon and cook for 15 more minutes.
5. Remove the bacon from the grill and let cool for 10 minutes before removing from the baking pan and serving.
6. Enjoy.

Nutrition Info: Calories 458, Total fat 14g, Saturated fat 10g, Total Carbs 37g, Net Carbs 37g, Protein 9g, Sugar 33g, Fiber 0g, Sodium: 565mg

162.   Deliciously Spicy Rack Of Lamb

Servings: 6
Cooking Time: 3 Hours
Ingredients:
- 2 tbsp. paprika
- ½ tbsp. coriander seeds
- 1 tsp. cumin seeds
- 1 tsp. ground allspice
- 1 tsp. lemon peel powder
- Salt and freshly ground black pepper, to taste
- 2 (1½-lb.) rack of lamb ribs, trimmed

Directions:
1. Set the temperature of Grill to 225 degrees F and preheat with closed lid for 15 minutes.
2. In a coffee grinder, add all ingredients except rib racks and grind into a powder.
3. Coat the rib racks with spice mixture generously.
4. Arrange the rib racks onto the grill and cook for about 3 hours.
5. Remove the rib racks from grill and place onto a cutting board for about 10-15 minutes before slicing.
6. With a sharp knife, cut the rib racks into equal-sized individual ribs and serve.

Nutrition Info: Calories per serving: 545; Carbohydrates: 1.7g; Protein: 64.4g; Fat: 29.7g; Sugar: 0.3g; Sodium: 221mg; Fiber: 1g

163.   Grilled Butter Basted Rib-eye

Servings: 4
Cooking Time: 20 Minutes
Ingredients:
- 2 rib-eye steaks, bone-in
- Slat to taste
- Pepper to taste
- 4 tbsp butter, unsalted

Directions:
1. Mix steak, salt, and pepper in a ziplock bag. Seal the bag and mix until the beef is well coated. Ensure you get as much air as possible from the ziplock bag.
2. Set the wood pellet grill temperature to high with closed lid for 15 minutes. Place a cast-iron into the grill.
3. Place the steaks on the hottest spot of the grill and cook for 5 minutes with the lid closed.
4. Open the lid and add butter to the skillet. When it's almost melted place the steak on the skillet with the grilled side up.
5. Cook for 5 minutes while busting the meat with butter. Close the lid and cook until the internal temperature is 130°F.
6. Remove the steak from skillet and let rest for 10 minutes before enjoying with the reserved butter.

Nutrition Info: Calories 745, Total fat 65g, Saturated fat 32g, Total Carbs 5g, Net Carbs 5g, Protein 35g, Sugar 0g, Fiber 0g

164. Pork Belly Burnt Ends

Servings: 8 To 10
Cooking Time: 6 Hours
Ingredients:
- 1 (3-pound) skinless pork belly (if not already skinned, use a sharp boning knife to remove the skin from the belly), cut into 1½- to 2-inch cubes
- 1 batch Sweet Brown Sugar Rub
- ½ cup honey
- 1 cup The Ultimate BBQ Sauce
- 2 tablespoons light brown sugar

Directions:
1. Supply your smoker with wood pellets and follow the manufacturer's specific start-up procedure. Preheat the grill, with the lid closed, to 250°F.
2. Generously season the pork belly cubes with the rub. Using your hands, work the rub into the meat.
3. Place the pork cubes directly on the grill grate and smoke until their internal temperature reaches 195°F.
4. Transfer the cubes from the grill to an aluminum pan. Add the honey, barbecue sauce, and brown sugar. Stir to combine and coat the pork.
5. Place the pan in the grill and smoke the pork for 1 hour, uncovered. Remove the pork from the grill and serve immediately.

165. Grilled Lamb Burgers

Servings: 5
Cooking Time: 15 Minutes
Ingredients:
- 1 1/4 pounds of ground lamb.
- 1 egg.
- 1 teaspoon of dried oregano.
- 1 teaspoon of dry sherry.
- 1 teaspoon of white wine vinegar.
- 4 minced cloves of garlic.
- Red pepper
- 1/2 cup of chopped green onions.
- 1 tablespoon of chopped mint.
- 2 tablespoons of chopped cilantro.
- 2 tablespoons of dry bread crumbs.
- 1/8 teaspoon of salt to taste.
- 1/4 teaspoon of ground black pepper to taste.
- 5 hamburger buns.

Directions:
1. Preheat a Wood Pellet Smoker or Grill to 350-450 degrees F then grease it grates. Using a large mixing bowl, add in all the ingredients on the list aside from the buns then mix properly to combine with clean hands. Make about five patties out of the mixture then set aside.
2. Place the lamb patties on the preheated grill and cook for about seven to nine minutes turning only once until an inserted thermometer reads 160 degrees F. Serve the lamb burgers on the hamburger, add your favorite toppings and enjoy.

Nutrition Info: Calories: 376 Cal Fat: 18.5 g Carbohydrates: 25.4 g Protein: 25.5 g Fiber: 1.6 g

166. Braised Lamb

Servings: 4
Cooking Time: 3 Hours And 20 Minutes
Ingredients:
- 4 lamb shanks
- Prime rib rub
- 1 cup red wine
- 1 cup beef broth
- 2 sprigs thyme
- 2 sprigs rosemary

Directions:
1. Sprinkle all sides of lamb shanks with prime rib rub.
2. Set temperature of the wood pellet grill to high.
3. Preheat it for 15 minutes while the lid is closed.
4. Add the lamb to the grill and cook for 20 minutes.
5. Transfer the lamb to a Dutch oven.
6. Stir in the rest of the ingredients.
7. Transfer back to the grill.
8. Reduce temperature to 325 degrees F.
9. Braise the lamb for 3 hours.
10. Tips: Let cool before serving.

167. Herby Lamb Chops

Servings: 4
Cooking Time: 2 Hours
Ingredients:
- 8 lamb chops, each about ¾-inch thick, fat trimmed
- For the Marinade:
- 1 teaspoon minced garlic
- Salt as needed
- 1 tablespoon dried rosemary
- Ground black pepper as needed
- ½ tablespoon dried thyme
- 3 tablespoons balsamic vinegar
- 1 tablespoon Dijon mustard
- ½ cup olive oil

Directions:
1. Prepare the marinade and for this, take a small bowl, place all of its ingredients in it and stir until well combined.
2. Place lamb chops in a large plastic bag, pour in marinade, seal the bag, turn it upside down to coat lamb chops with the marinade and let it marinate for a minimum of 4 hours in the refrigerator.
3. When ready to cook, switch on the grill, fill the grill hopper with flavored wood pellets, power the grill on by using the control panel, select 'smoke' on the temperature dial, or set the temperature to 450 degrees F and let it preheat for a minimum of 5 minutes.
4. Meanwhile, remove lamb chops from the refrigerator and bring them to room temperature.
5. When the grill has preheated, open the lid, place lamb chops on the grill grate, shut the grill and smoke for 5 minutes per side until seared.
6. When done, transfer lamb chops to a dish, let them rest for 5 minutes and then serve.
Nutrition Info: Calories: 280 Cal ;Fat: 12.3 g ;Carbs: 8.3 g ;Protein: 32.7 g ;Fiber: 1.2 g

168.   Versatile Beef Tenderloin

Servings: 6
Cooking Time: 2 Hours 5 Minutes
Ingredients:
- For Brandy Butter:
- ½ C. butter
- 1 oz. brandy
- For Brandy Sauce:
- 2 oz. brandy
- 8 garlic cloves, minced
- ¼ C. mixed fresh herbs (parsley, rosemary and thyme), chopped
- 2 tsp. honey
- 2 tsp. hot English mustard
- For Tenderloin:
- 1 (2-lb.) center-cut beef tenderloin
- Salt and cracked black peppercorns, to taste

Directions:
1. Set the temperature of Grill to 230 degrees F and preheat with closed lid for 15 minutes.
2. For brandy butter: in a pan, melt butter over medium-low heat.
3. Stir in brandy and remove from heat.
4. Set aside, covered to keep warm.
5. For brandy sauce: in a bowl, add all ingredients and mix until well combined.
6. Season the tenderloin with salt and black peppercorns generously.
7. Coat tenderloin with brandy sauce evenly.
8. With a baster-injector, inject tenderloin with brandy butter.
9. Place the tenderloin onto the grill and cook for about 1½-2 hours, injecting with brandy butter occasionally.
10. Remove the tenderloin from grill and place onto a cutting board for about 10-15 minutes before serving.
11. With a sharp knife, cut the tenderloin into desired-sized slices and serve.

Nutrition Info: Calories per serving: 496; Carbohydrates: 4.4g; Protein: 44.4g; Fat: 29.3g; Sugar: 2g; Sodium: 240mg; Fiber: 0.7g

169.   Pastrami

Servings: 6 To 8
Cooking Time: 12 To 16 Hours
Ingredients:
- 1 (8-pound) corned beef brisket
- 2 tablespoons yellow mustard
- 1 batch Espresso Brisket Rub
- Worcestershire Mop and Spritz, for spritzing

Directions:
1. Supply your with wood pellets and follow the start-up procedure. Preheat the grill, with the lid closed, to 225°F.
2. Coat the brisket all over with mustard and season it with the rub. Using your hands, work the rub into the meat. Pour the mop into a spray bottle.
3. Place the brisket directly on the grill grate and smoke until its internal temperature reaches 195°F, spritzing it every hour with the mop.
4. Pull the corned beef brisket from the grill and wrap it completely in aluminum foil or butcher paper. Place the wrapped brisket in a cooler, cover the cooler, and let it rest for 1 or 2 hours.
5. Remove the corned beef from the cooler and unwrap it. Slice the corned beef and serve.

170.   Tri-tip

Servings: 6
Cooking Time: 1 Hour 30 Minutes;
Ingredients:
- 3 lb tri-tip
- 1-1/2 tbsp kosher salt
- 1 tbsp black pepper
- 1 tbsp paprika
- 1/2 tbsp cayenne
- 1 tbsp onion powder
- 1 tbsp garlic powder

Directions:
1. Preheat your to 250F.
2. Mix the seasoning ingredients and generously season the tri-tip.
3. Place it in the and cook for 30 minutes. Flip the tri-tip and cook for an additional 30 minutes.
4. Turn up the and coo for additional 30 minutes. Pull out the meat at 125F for medium-rare and 135F for medium.
5. Let the meat rest for 10 minutes before slicing and serving.

Nutrition Info: Calories 484, Total fat 25g, Saturated fat 0g, Total carbs 1g, Net carbs 1g Protein 59g, Sugars 0g, Fiber 0g, Sodium 650mmg

171.   Rosemary Prime Rib

Servings: 8
Cooking Time: 1 Hour
Ingredients:
- 8 pounds whole ribeye roast
- 4 tablespoons olive oil
- 4 tablespoons peppercorns
- 3 whole rosemary sprigs
- ½ cup garlic, minced
- ½ cup smoked salt

Directions:
1. Fire the Grill to 500F. Use desired wood pellets when cooking. Close the lid and preheat for 15 minutes.
2. Cut the rib loin in half and sear the halves in oil over high heat until golden brown. Set aside.
3. Place the peppercorns in a bag and crush with a rolling pin. Next, strip the rosemary leaves from the stem and mix with garlic and salt.
4. Season the seared steak with the spice mixture.
5. Place in the grill and roast for 30 minutes and reduce the heat to 300F. Cook for another 30 minutes.
6. Once cooked, remove from the grill, and allow to rest for 20 minutes before slicing.

Nutrition Info: Calories per serving: 954; Protein: 128.5g; Carbs: 4.1g; Fat: 47.7g Sugar: 0.3g

172.   Bacon Stuffed Smoked Pork Loin

Servings: 4 To 6
Cooking Time: 1 Hour
Ingredients:
- 3 Pound Pork Loin, Butterflied
- As Needed Pork Rub
- 1/4 Cup Walnuts, Chopped
- 1/3 Cup Craisins
- 1 Tablespoon Oregano, fresh
- 1 Tablespoon fresh thyme
- 6 Pieces Asparagus, fresh
- 6 Slices Bacon, sliced
- 1/3 Cup Parmesan cheese, grated
- As Needed Bacon Grease

Directions:
1. Lay down 2 large pieces of butcher's twine on your work surface. Place butterflied pork loin perpendicular to twine.
2. Season the inside of the pork loin with the pork rub.
3. On one end of the loin, layer in a line all of the ingredients, beginning with the chopped walnuts, craisins, oregano, thyme, and asparagus.
4. Add bacon and top with the parmesan cheese.
5. Starting at the end with all of the fillings, carefully roll up the pork loin and secure on both ends with butcher's twine.
6. Roll the pork loin in the reserved bacon grease and season the outside with more Pork Rub.
7. When ready to cook, set temperature to 180°F and preheat, lid closed for 15 minutes. Place stuffed pork loin directly on the grill grate and smoke for 1 hour.
8. Remove the pork loin; increase the temperature to 350°F and allow to preheat.
9. Place the loin back on the and grill for approximately 30 to 45 minutes or until the temperature reads 135°F on an instant-read thermometer.
10. Move the pork loin to a plate and tent it with aluminum foil. Let it rest for 15 minutes before slicing and serving. Enjoy!

173.   Grilled Lamb With Sugar Glaze

Servings: 4
Cooking Time: 20 Minutes
Ingredients:
- 1/4 cup sugar
- 2 tbsp ground ginger
- 2 tbsp dried tarragon
- 1/2 tbsp salt
- 1 tbsp black pepper, ground
- 1 tbsp ground cinnamon
- 1 tbsp garlic powder
- 4 lamb chops

Directions:
1. In a mixing bowl, mix sugar, ground ginger, tarragon, salt, pepper, cinnamon, and garlic.
2. Rub the lamb chops with the mixture and refrigerate for an hour.
3. Meanwhile, preheat your Traeger.
4. Brush the grill grates with oil and place the marinated lamb chops on it. Cook for 5 minutes on each side.
5. Serve and enjoy.
Nutrition Info: Calories 241, Total fat 13.1g, Saturated fat 5.6g, Total carbs 15.8g, Net carbs 15.1g Protein 14.6g, Sugars 13.6g, Fiber 0.7g, Sodium 339.2mg, Potassium 256.7mg

174.   St. Patrick Day's Corned Beef

Servings: 14
Cooking Time: 7 Hours
Ingredients:
- 6 lb. corned beef brisket, drained, rinsed and pat dried
- Freshly ground black pepper, to taste
- 8 oz. light beer

Directions:
1. Set the temperature of Grill to 275 degrees F and preheat with closed lid for 15 minutes.
2. Sprinkle the beef brisket with spice packet evenly.
3. Now, sprinkle the brisket with black pepper lightly.
4. Place the brisket onto the grill and cook for about 3-4 hours.
5. Remove from grill and transfer briskets into an aluminum pan.
6. Add enough beer just to cover the bottom of pan.
7. With a piece of foil, cover the pan, leaving one corner open to let out steam.
8. Cook for about 2-3 hours.
9. Remove the brisket from grill and place onto a cutting board for about 10-15 minutes before slicing.
10. With a sharp knife, cut the brisket in desired sized slices and serve.
11. Remove the brisket from grill and place onto a cutting board for about 25-30 minutes before slicing.
12. With a sharp knife, cut the brisket in desired sized slices and serve.

Nutrition Info: Calories per serving: 337; Carbohydrates: 0.6g; Protein: 26.1g; Fat: 24.3g; Sugar: 0g; Sodium: 1719mg; Fiber: 0g

175.   Wood Pellet Grilled Tenderloin With Fresh Herb Sauce

Servings: 4
Cooking Time: 15 Minutes
Ingredients:
- Pork
- 1 pork tenderloin, silver skin removed and dried
- BBQ seasoning
- Fresh herb sauce
- 1 handful basil, fresh
- 1/4 tbsp garlic powder
- 1/3 cup olive oil
- 1/2 tbsp kosher salt

Directions:
1. Preheat the wood pellet grill to medium heat.
2. Coat the pork with BBQ seasoning then cook on semi-direct heat of the grill. Turn the pork regularly to ensure even cooking.
3. Cook until the internal temperature is 145°F. Remove from the grill and let it rest for 10 minutes.
4. Meanwhile, make the herb sauce by pulsing all the sauce ingredients in a food processor. Pulse for a few times or until well chopped.
5. Slice the pork diagonally and spoon the sauce on top. Serve and enjoy.

Nutrition Info: Calories 300, Total fat 22g, Saturated fat 4g, Total Carbs 13g, Net Carbs 12g, Protein 14g, Sugar 10g, Fiber 1g, Sodium: 791mg

176. Homemade Meatballs

Servings: 12
Cooking Time: 1 Hour 20 Minutes
Ingredients:
- Ground beef - 2 lbs
- White bread - 2 slices
- Whole milk - ½ cup
- Salt - 1 tbsp
- Onion powder - ½ tbsp
- Italian seasoning - 2 tbsp
- Ground black pepper- ¼ tbsp
- Minced garlic - ½ tbsp

Directions:
1. Combine the whole milk, white bread, minced garlic, onion powder, Italian seasoning, and black pepper.
2. Add the ground beef and mix well.
3. Preheat your wood pellet grill on the 'smoke' option and leave the lid open for 4-5 minutes.
4. Line a baking sheet and start placing small balls on the sheet.
5. Smoke for 35 minutes and then flip the balls.
6. Let it stay for 35 more minutes.
7. Once it turns golden brown, serve hot!

Nutrition Info: Carbohydrates: 7 g Protein: 42 g Fat: 27 g Sodium: 550 mg Cholesterol: 137 mg

177. Apple Bourbon Glazed Ham

Servings: 6
Cooking Time: 60 Minutes
Ingredients:
- 1 cup apple jelly
- 2 tablespoons Dijon mustard
- 2 tablespoons bourbon
- 2 tablespoons lemon juice
- ½ teaspoon ground cloves
- 2 cups apple juice
- 1 large ham

Directions:
1. Fire the Grill to 500F. Use maple wood pellets when cooking. Close the lid and preheat for 15 minutes.
2. In a small saucepan, combine the apple jelly, mustard, bourbon, lemon juice, cloves, and apple juice. Cook on low heat to melt the apple jelly. Cook for 5 minutes and set aside.
3. Place the ham in a baking tray and glaze with the reserved mixture.
4. Place on the grill rack and cook for 60 minutes.
5. Once the ham is cooked, remove from the grill, and allow to rest for 20 minutes before slicing.
6. Pour over the remaining glaze.

Nutrition Info: Calories per serving: 283; Protein: 38.7 g; Carbs: 14.7g; Fat: 8g Sugar: 10g

178. Teriyaki Pork Tenderloin

Servings: 12 To 15
Cooking Time: 1½ To 2 Hours
Ingredients:
- 2 (1-pound) pork tenderloins
- 1 batch Quick and Easy Teriyaki Marinade
- Smoked salt

Directions:
1. In a large zip-top bag, combine the tenderloins and marinade. Seal the bag, turn to coat, and refrigerate the pork for at least 30 minutes—I recommend up to overnight.
2. Supply your smoker with wood pellets and follow the manufacturer's specific start-up procedure. Preheat the grill, with the lid closed, to 180°F.
3. Remove the tenderloins from the marinade and season them with smoked salt.
4. Place the tenderloins directly on the grill grate and smoke for 1 hour.
5. Increase the grill's temperature to 300°F and continue to cook until the pork's internal temperature reaches 145°F.
6. Remove the tenderloins from the grill and let them rest for 5 to 10 minutes, before thinly slicing and serving.

179. Restaurant-style Rib-eye Steak

Servings: 2
Cooking Time: 20 Minutes
Ingredients:
- 2 (1 3/8-inch thick) rib-eye steaks, trimmed
- 1 tbsp. olive oil
- 1 tbsp. steak seasoning

Directions:
1. Coat both sides of each steak with oil and season with steak seasoning.
2. Set aside at room temperature for about 15 minutes.
3. Set the temperature of Grill to 325 degrees F and preheat with closed lid for 15 minutes.
4. Place the steaks onto the grill and cook for about 15-20 minutes, flipping after every 6 minutes.
5. Remove from grill and serve immediately.
Nutrition Info: Calories per serving: 527; Carbohydrates: 0g; Protein: 30.1g; Fat: 44.6; Sugar: 0g; Sodium: 98mg; Fiber: 0g

180. Wood Pellet Grill Teriyaki Beef Jerky

Servings: 10
Cooking Time: 5 Hours
Ingredients:
- 3 cups soy sauce
- 2 cups brown sugar
- 3 garlic cloves
- 2-inch ginger knob, peeled and chopped
- 1 tbsp sesame oil
- 4 lb beef, skirt steak

Directions:
1. Place all the ingredients except the meat in a food processor. Pulse until well mixed.
2. Trim any excess fat from the meat and slice into 1/4 inch slices. Add the steak with the marinade into a zip lock bag and let marinate for 12-24 hours in a fridge.
3. Set the wood pellet grill to smoke and let preheat for 5 minutes.
4. Arrange the steaks on the grill leaving a space between each. Let smoke for 5 hours.
5. Remove the steak from grill and serve when warm.
Nutrition Info: Calories 80, Total fat 1g, Saturated fat 0g, Total Carbs 7g, Net Carbs 0g, Protein 11g, Sugar 6g, Fiber 0g, Sodium: 390mg

181.   Wood Pellet Grill Dale's Lamb

Servings: 8
Cooking Time: 50 Minutes
Ingredients:
- 2/3 cup lemon juice
- 1/2 cup brown sugar
- 1/4 cup Dijon mustard
- 1/4 cup soy sauce
- 1/4 cup olive oil
- 2 garlic cloves, minced
- 1 piece ginger root, freshly sliced
- 1 tbsp salt
- 1/2 tbsp black pepper, ground
- 5 lb leg of lamb, butterflied

Directions:
1. In a mixing bowl, mix lemon juice, sugar, dijon mustard, sauce, oil, garlic cloves, ginger root, salt, and pepper.
2. Place the lamb in a dish and pour the seasoning mixture over it. Cover the dish and put in a fridge to marinate for 8 hours.
3. Preheat a wood pellet grill to medium heat. Drain the marinade from the dish and bring it to boil in a small saucepan.
4. Reduce heat and let simmer while whisking occasionally.
5. Oil the grill grate and place the lamb on it. Cook for 50 minutes or until the internal temperature reaches 145 F while turning occasionally.
6. Slice the lamb and cover with the marinade. Serve and enjoy.

Nutrition Info: Calories 451, Total fat 27.2g, Saturated fat 9.5g, Total Carbs 17.8g, Net Carbs 17.6g, Protein 32.4g, Sugar 14g, Fiber 0.2g, Sodium: 1015mg, Potassium 455mg.

182.   Wood Pellet Smoked Beef Jerky

Servings: 10
Cooking Time: 5 Hours
Ingredients:
- 3 lb sirloin steaks, sliced into 1/4 inch thickness
- 2 cups soy sauce
- 1/2 cup brown sugar
- 1 cup pineapple juice
- 2 tbsp sriracha
- 2 tbsp red pepper flake
- 2 tbsp hoisin
- 2 tbsp onion powder
- 2 tbsp rice wine vinegar
- 2 tbsp garlic, minced

Directions:
1. Mix all the ingredients in a ziplock bag. Seal the bag and mix until the beef is well coated. Ensure you get as much air as possible from the ziplock bag.
2. Put the bag in the fridge overnight to let marinate. Remove the bag from the fridge 1 hour prior to cooking.
3. Startup your wood pallet grill and set it to smoke setting. Layout the meat on the grill with half-inch space between them.
4. Let them cook for 5 hours while turning after every 2-1/2 hours.
5. Transfer from the grill and let cool for 30 minutes before serving.
6. enjoy.

Nutrition Info: Calories 80, Total fat 1g, Saturated fat 0g, Total carbs 5g, Net carbs 5g, Protein 14g, Sugar 5g, Fiber 0g, Sodium: 650mg

183.   Wood Pellet Togarashi Pork Tenderloin

Servings: 6
Cooking Time: 25 Minutes
Ingredients:
- 1 Pork tenderloin
- 1/2tbsp kosher salt
- 1/4 cup Togarashi seasoning

Directions:
1.   Cut any excess silver skin from the pork and sprinkle with salt to taste. Rub generously with the togarashi seasoning
2.   Place in a preheated oven at 400°F for 25 minutes or until the internal temperature reaches 145°F.
3.   Remove from the grill and let rest for 10 minutes before slicing and serving.
4.   Enjoy.

Nutrition Info: Calories 390, Total fat 13g, Saturated fat 6g, Total Carbs 4g, Net Carbs 1g, Protein 33g, Sugar 0g, Fiber 3g, Sodium: 66mg

184.   Roasted Venison Tenderloin

Servings: 4
Cooking Time: 20 Minutes
Ingredients:
- 2 pounds venison
- ¼ cup dry red wine
- 2 cloves garlic, minced
- 2 tablespoons soy sauce
- 1 ½ tablespoons red wine vinegar
- 1 tablespoon rosemary
- 1 teaspoon black pepper
- ½ cup olive oil
- Salt to taste

Directions:
1.   Remove the membrane covering the venison. Set aside.
2.   Mix the rest of the ingredients in a bowl. Place the venison in the bowl and allow to marinate for at least 5 hours in the fridge.
3.   Fire the Grill to 500F. Use desired wood pellets when cooking. Close the lid and preheat for 15 minutes.
4.   Remove the venison from the marinade and pat dry using a paper towel.
5.   Place on the grill grate and cook for 10 minutes on each side for medium rare.

Nutrition Info: Calories per serving: 611 ; Protein: 68.4g; Carbs: 3.1g; Fat: 34.4g Sugar: 1.6g

185.   Buttered Tenderloin

Servings: 8
Cooking Time: 45 Minutes
Ingredients:
- 1 (4-lb.) beef tenderloin, trimmed
- Smoked salt and cracked black pepper, to taste
- 3 tbsp. butter, melted

Directions:
1.   Set the temperature of Grill to 300 degrees F and preheat with closed lid for 15 minutes.
2.   Season the tenderloin with salt and black pepper generously and then rub with butter.
3.   Place the tenderloin onto the grill and cook for about 45 minutes.
4.   Remove the tenderloin from grill and place onto a cutting board for about 10-15 minutes before serving.
5.   With a sharp knife, cut the tenderloin into desired-sized slices and serve.

Nutrition Info: Calories per serving: 505; Carbohydrates: 0g; Protein: 65.7g; Fat: 25.1g; Sugar: 0g; Sodium: 184mg; Fiber: 0g

186. Crown Rack Of Lamb

Servings: 6
Cooking Time: 30 Minutes
Ingredients:
- 2 racks of lamb. Frenched
- 1 tbsp garlic, crushed
- 1 tbsp rosemary
- 1/2 cup olive oil
- Kitchen twine

Directions:
1. Preheat your to 450F.
2. Rinse the lab with clean cold water then pat it dry with a paper towel.
3. Lay the lamb flat on a chopping board and score a ¼ inch down between the bones. Repeat the process between the bones on each lamb rack. Set aside.
4. In a small mixing bowl, combine garlic, rosemary, and oil. Brush the lamb of rack generously with the mixture.
5. Bend the lamb rack into a semicircle then place the racks together such that the bones will be up and will form a crown shape.
6. Wrap around 4 times starting from the base moving upward. Tie tightly to keep the racks together.
7. Place the lambs on a baking sheet and set in the Traeger. Cook on high heat for 10 minutes. Reduce the temperature to 300F and cook for 20 more minutes or until the internal temperature reaches 130F.
8. Remove the lamb rack from the and let rest while wrapped in a foil for 15 minutes.
9. Serve when hot.
Nutrition Info: Calories 390, Total fat 35g, Saturated fat 15g, Total carbs 0g, Net carbs 0g Protein 17g, Sugars 0g, Fiber 0g, Sodium 65mg

187. Cowboy Cut Steak

Servings: 4
Cooking Time: 1 Hour And 15 Minutes
Ingredients:
- 2 cowboy cut steak, each about 2 ½ pounds
- Salt as needed
- Beef rub as needed
- For the Gremolata:
- 2 tablespoons chopped mint
- 1 bunch of parsley, leaves separated
- 1 lemon, juiced
- 1 tablespoon lemon zest
- ½ teaspoon minced garlic
- ¼ teaspoon salt
- 1/8 teaspoon ground black pepper
- 1/4 cup olive oil

Directions:
1. Switch on the grill, fill the grill hopper with mesquite flavored wood pellets, power the grill on by using the control panel, select 'smoke' on the temperature dial, or set the temperature to 225 degrees F and let it preheat for a minimum of 5 minutes.
2. Meanwhile, prepare the steaks, and for this, season them with salt and BBQ rub until well coated.
3. When the grill has preheated, open the lid, place steaks on the grill grate, shut the grill and smoke for 45 minutes to 1 hour until thoroughly cooked, and internal temperature reaches 115 degrees F.
4. Meanwhile, prepare gremolata and for this, take a medium bowl, place all of its ingredients in it and then stir well until combined, set aside until combined.
5. When done, transfer steaks to a dish, let rest for 15 minutes, and meanwhile, change the smoking temperature of the grill to 450 degrees F and let it preheat for a minimum of 10 minutes.
6. Then return steaks to the grill grate and cook for 7 minutes per side until the internal temperature reaches 130 degrees F.
Nutrition Info: Calories: 361 Cal ;Fat: 31 g ;Carbs: 1 g ;Protein: 19 g ;Fiber: 0.2 g

188.   Smoked, Candied, And Spicy Bacon

Servings: 10
Cooking Time: 40 Minutes
Ingredients:
- Center-cut bacon - 1 lb.
- Brown sugar - ½ cup
- Maple syrup - ½ cup
- Hot sauce - 1 tbsp
- Pepper - ½ tbsp

Directions:
1. Mix the maple syrup, brown sugar, hot sauce, and pepper in a bowl.
2. Preheat your wood pellet grill to 300 degrees.
3. Line a baking sheet and place the bacon slices on it.
4. Generously spread the brown sugar mix on both sides of the bacon slices.
5. Place the pan on the wood pellet grill for 20 minutes. Flip the bacon pieces.
6. Leave them for another 15 minutes until the bacon looks cooked, and the sugar is melted.
7. Remove from the grill and let it stay for 10-15 minutes.
8. Voila! Your bacon candy is ready!

Nutrition Info: Carbohydrates: 37 g Protein: 9 g Sodium: 565 mg Cholesterol: 49 mg

189.   Maple Baby Backs

Servings: 4 To 6
Cooking Time: 4 Hours
Ingredients:
- 2 (2- or 3-pound) racks baby back ribs
- 2 tablespoons yellow mustard
- 1 batch Sweet Brown Sugar Rub
- ½ cup plus 2 tablespoons maple syrup, divided
- 2 tablespoons light brown sugar
- 1 cup Pepsi or other non-diet cola
- ¼ cup The Ultimate BBQ Sauce

Directions:
1. Supply your smoker with wood pellets and follow the manufacturer's specific start-up procedure. Preheat the grill, with the lid closed, to 180°F.
2. Remove the membrane from the backside of the ribs. This can be done by cutting just through the membrane in an X pattern and working a paper towel between the membrane and the ribs to pull it off.
3. Coat the ribs on both sides with mustard and season them with the rub. Using your hands, work the rub into the meat.
4. Place the ribs directly on the grill grate and smoke for 3 hours.
5. Remove the ribs from the grill and place them, bone-side up, on enough aluminum foil to wrap the ribs completely. Drizzle 2 tablespoons of maple syrup over the ribs and sprinkle them with 1 tablespoon of brown sugar. Flip the ribs and repeat the maple syrup and brown sugar application on the meat side.
6. Increase the grill's temperature to 300°F.
7. Fold in three sides of the foil around the ribs and add the cola. Fold in the last side, completely enclosing the ribs and liquid. Return the ribs to the grill and cook for 30 to 45 minutes.
8. Remove the ribs from the grill and unwrap them from the foil.
9. In a small bowl, stir together the barbecue sauce and remaining 6 tablespoons of maple syrup. Use this to baste the ribs. Return the ribs to the grill, without the foil, and cook for 15 minutes to caramelize the sauce.
10. Cut into individual ribs and serve immediately.

190.   Brown Sugar Lamb Chops

Servings: 4
Cooking Time: 10-15 Minutes
Ingredients:
- Pepper
- One t. garlic powder
- Salt
- Two t. tarragon
- One t. cinnamon
- ¼ c. brown sugar
- 4 lamb chops
- Two t. ginger

Directions:
1.   Combine the salt, garlic powder, pepper, cinnamon, tarragon, ginger, and sugar. Coat the lamb chops in the mixture and chill for two hours.
2.   Add wood pellets to your smoker and follow your cooker's startup procedure. Preheat your smoker, with your lid closed, until it reaches 450. Place the chops on the grill, cover, and smoke for 10-15 minutes per side. Serve.

Nutrition Info: Calories: 210 Cal Fat: 11 g Carbohydrates: 3 g   Protein: 25 g Fiber: 1 g

191.   Smoked Apple Bbq Ribs

Servings: 6
Cooking Time: 2 Hours
Ingredients:
- 2 racks St. Louis-style ribs
- ¼ cup Big Game Rub
- 1 cup apple juice
- A bottle of BBQ Sauce

Directions:
1.   Place the ribs on a working surface and remove the film of connective tissues covering it.
2.   In another bowl, mix the Game Rub and apple juice until well-combined.
3.   Massage the rub on to the ribs and allow to rest in the fridge for at least 2 hours.
4.   When ready to cook, fire the Grill to 225F. Use apple wood pellets when cooking the ribs. Close the lid and preheat for 15 minutes.
5.   Place the ribs on the grill grate and close the lid. Smoke for 1 hour and 30 minutes. Make sure to flip the ribs halfway through the cooking time.
6.   Ten minutes before the cooking time ends, brush the ribs with BBQ sauce.
7.   Remove from the grill and allow to rest before slicing.

Nutrition Info: Calories per serving: 337 ; Protein: 47.1g; Carbs: 4.7 g; Fat: 12.9g Sugar: 4g

192.   Lamb Leg With Salsa

Servings: 6
Cooking Time: 1 Hour And 30 Minutes
Ingredients:
- 6 cloves garlic, peeled and sliced
- 1 leg of lamb
- Salt and pepper to taste
- 2 tablespoons fresh rosemary, chopped
- Olive oil
- 3 cups salsa

Directions:
1. Set the wood pellet grill to high.
2. Preheat for 15 minutes while the lid is closed.
3. Make slits all over the lamb leg.
4. Insert the garlic slices.
5. Drizzle with oil and rub with salt, pepper and rosemary.
6. Marinate for 30 minutes.
7. Set temperature to 350 degrees F.
8. Cook lamb leg for 1 hour and 30 minutes.
9. Serve with salsa.
10. Tips: You can also insert whole garlic cloves into the slits.

193.   Jalapeño-bacon Pork Tenderloin

Servings: 4 To 6
Cooking Time: 2 Hours And 30 Minutes
Ingredients:
- ¼ cup yellow mustard
- 2 (1-pound) pork tenderloins
- ¼ cup Pork Rub
- 8 ounces cream cheese, softened
- 1 cup grated Cheddar cheese
- 1 tablespoon unsalted butter, melted
- 1 tablespoon minced garlic
- 2 jalapeño peppers, seeded and diced
- 1½ pounds bacon

Directions:
1. Slather the mustard all over the pork tenderloins, then sprinkle generously with the dry rub to coat the meat.
2. Supply your smoker with wood pellets and follow the manufacturer's specific start-up procedure. Preheat, with the lid closed, to 225°F.
3. Place the tenderloins directly on the grill, close the lid, and smoke for 2 hours.
4. Remove the pork from the grill and increase the temperature to 375°F.
5. In a small bowl, combine the cream cheese, Cheddar cheese, melted butter, garlic, and jalapeños.
6. Starting from the top, slice deeply along the center of each tenderloin end to end, creating a cavity.
7. Spread half of the cream cheese mixture in the cavity of one tenderloin. Repeat with the remaining mixture and the other piece of meat.
8. Securely wrap one tenderloin with half of the bacon. Repeat with the remaining bacon and the other piece of meat.
9. Transfer the bacon-wrapped tenderloins to the grill, close the lid, and smoke for about 30 minutes, or until a meat thermometer inserted in the thickest part of the meat reads 160°F and the bacon is browned and cooked through.
10. Let the tenderloins rest for 5 to 10 minutes before slicing and serving.

194.   Smoked Roast Beef

Servings: 5 To 8
Cooking Time: 12 To 14 Hours
Ingredients:
- 1 (4-pound) top round roast
- 1 batch Espresso Brisket Rub
- 1 tablespoon butter

Directions:
1.   Supply your with wood pellets and follow the start-up procedure. Preheat the grill, with the lid closed, to 180°F.
2.   Season the top round roast with the rub. Using your hands, work the rub into the meat.
3.   Place the roast directly on the grill grate and smoke until its internal temperature reaches 140°F. Remove the roast from the grill.
4.   Place a cast-iron skillet on the grill grate and increase the grill's temperature to 450°F. Place the roast in the skillet, add the butter, and cook until its internal temperature reaches 145°F, flipping once after about 3 minutes.
5.   Remove the roast from the grill and let it rest for 10 to 15 minutes, before slicing and serving.

195.   The Perfect T-bones

Servings: 4
Cooking Time: 30 Minutes
Ingredients:
- 4 (1½- to 2-inch-thick) T-bone steaks
- 2 tablespoons olive oil
- 1 batch Espresso Brisket Rub or Chili-Coffee Rub

Directions:
1.   Supply your with wood pellets and follow the start-up procedure. Preheat the grill, with the lid closed, to 500°F.
2.   Coat the steaks all over with olive oil and season both sides with the rub. Using your hands, work the rub into the meat.
3.   Place the steaks directly on a grill grate and smoke until their internal temperature reaches 135°F for rare, 145°F for medium-rare, and 155°F for well-done. Remove the steaks from the grill and serve hot.

VEGETABLE & VEGETARIAN RECIPES

196. Wood Pellet Grilled Asparagus And Honey Glazed Carrots

Servings: 5
Cooking Time: 35 Minutes
Ingredients:
- 1 bunch asparagus, trimmed ends
- 1 lb carrots, peeled
- 2 tbsp olive oil
- Sea salt to taste
- 2 tbsp honey
- Lemon zest

Directions:
1. Sprinkle the asparagus with oil and sea salt. Drizzle the carrots with honey and salt.
2. Preheat the wood pellet to 165°F wit the lid closed for 15 minutes.
3. Place the carrots in the wood pellet and cook for 15 minutes. Add asparagus and cook for 20 more minutes or until cooked through.
4. Top the carrots and asparagus with lemon zest. Enjoy.

Nutrition Info: Calories 1680, Total fat 30g, Saturated fat 2g, Total Carbs 10g, Net Carbs 10g, Protein 4g, Sugar 0g, Fiber 0g, Sodium: 514mg, Potassium 0mg

197. Smoked Baked Beans

Servings: 12
Cooking Time: 3 Hours
Ingredients:
- 1 medium yellow onion diced
- 3 jalapenos
- 56 oz pork and beans
- 3/4 cup barbeque sauce
- 1/2 cup dark brown sugar
- 1/4 cup apple cider vinegar
- 2 tbsp Dijon mustard
- 2 tbsp molasses

Directions:
1. Preheat the smoker to 250°F. Pour the beans along with all the liquid in a pan. Add brown sugar, barbeque sauce, Dijon mustard, apple cider vinegar, and molasses. Stir. Place the pan on one of the racks. Smoke for 3 hours until thickened. Remove after 3 hours. Serve

Nutrition Info: Calories: 214 Cal Fat: 2 g Carbohydrates: 42 g   Protein: 7 g Fiber: 7 g

198.   Split Pea Soup With Mushrooms

Servings: 4
Cooking Time: 35 Minutes
Ingredients:
- 2tbsp. Olive Oil
- 3Garlic cloves, minced
- 3tbsp. Parsley, fresh and chopped
- 2Carrots chopped
- 1.2/3 cup Green Peas
- 9cups Water
- 2tsp. Salt
- 1/4 tsp. Black Pepper
- 1lb. Portobello Mushrooms
- 1Bay Leaf
- 2Celery Ribs, chopped
- 1Onion quartered
- 1/2 tsp. Thyme, dried
- 6tbsp. Parmesan Cheese, grated

Directions:
1. First, keep oil, onion, and garlic in the blender pitcher.
2. Next, select the 'saute' button.
3. Once sautéed, stir in the rest of the ingredients, excluding parsley and cheese.
4. Then, press the 'hearty soup' button.
5. Finally, transfer the soup among the serving bowls and garnish it with parsley and cheese.

Nutrition Info: Calories: 61 Fat: 1.1 g Total Carbs: 10 g Fiber: 1.9 g Sugar: 3.2 g Protein: 3.2 g Cholesterol: 0

199.   Baked Parmesan Mushrooms

Servings: 8
Cooking Time: 15 Minutes
Ingredients:
- 8 mushroom caps
- 1/2 cup Parmesan cheese, grated
- 1/2 teaspoon garlic salt
- 1/4 cup mayonnaise
- Pinch paprika
- Hot sauce

Directions:
1. Place mushroom caps in a baking pan.
2. Mix the remaining ingredients in a bowl.
3. Scoop the mixture onto the mushroom.
4. Place the baking pan on the grill.
5. Cook in the wood pellet grill at 350 degrees F for 15 minutes while the lid is closed.
6. Tips: You can also add chopped sausage to the mixture.

200.   Smoked Balsamic Potatoes And Carrots

Servings: 6
Cooking Time: 10 Minutes
Ingredients:
- 2 large carrots, peeled and chopped roughly
- 2 large Yukon Gold potatoes, peeled and wedged
- 5 tablespoons olive oil
- 5 tablespoons balsamic vinegar
- Salt and pepper to taste

Directions:
1. Fire the Grill to 400F. Use desired wood pellets when cooking. Close the lid and preheat for 15 minutes.
2. Place all ingredients in a bowl and toss to coat the vegetables with the seasoning.
3. Place on a baking tray lined with foil.
4. Place on the grill grate and close the lid. Cook for 30 minutes.

Nutrition Info: Calories per serving: 219; Protein: 2.9g; Carbs: 27g; Fat: 11.4g Sugar:4.5 g

201. Smoked Brussels Sprouts

Servings: 6
Cooking Time: 45 Minutes
Ingredients:
- 1-1/2 pounds Brussels sprouts
- 2 cloves of garlic minced
- 2 tbsp extra virgin olive oil
- Sea salt and cracked black pepper

Directions:
1. Rinse sprouts
2. Remove the outer leaves and brown bottoms off the sprouts.
3. Place sprouts in a large bowl then coat with olive oil.
4. Add a coat of garlic, salt, and pepper and transfer them to the pan.
5. Add to the top rack of the smoker with water and woodchips.
6. Smoke for 45 minutes or until reaches 250°F temperature.
7. Serve

Nutrition Info: Calories: 84 Cal Fat: 4.9 g Carbohydrates: 7.2 g Protein: 2.6 g Fiber: 2.9 g

202. Roasted Green Beans With Bacon

Servings: 6
Cooking Time: 20 Minutes
Ingredients:
- 1-pound green beans
- 4 strips bacon, cut into small pieces
- 4 tablespoons extra virgin olive oil
- 2 cloves garlic, minced
- 1 teaspoon salt

Directions:
1. Fire the Grill to 400F. Use desired wood pellets when cooking. Close the lid and preheat for 15 minutes.
2. Toss all ingredients on a sheet tray and spread out evenly.
3. Place the tray on the grill grate and roast for 20 minutes.

Nutrition Info: Calories per serving: 65 ; Protein: 1.3g; Carbs: 3.8g; Fat: 5.3g Sugar: 0.6g

203. Smoked Watermelon

Servings: 5
Cooking Time: 45-90 Minutes
Ingredients:
- 1 small seedless watermelon
- Balsamic vinegar
- Wooden skewers

Directions:
1. Slice ends of small seedless watermelons
2. Slice the watermelon in 1-inch cubes. Put the cubes in a container and drizzle vinegar on the cubes of watermelon.
3. Preheat the smoker to 225°F. Add wood chips and water to the smoker before starting preheating.
4. Place the cubes on the skewers.
5. Place the skewers on the smoker rack for 50 minutes.
6. Cook
7. Remove the skewers.
8. Serve!

Nutrition Info: Calories: 20 Cal Fat: 0 g Carbohydrates: 4 g Protein: 1 g Fiber: 0.2 g

204.   Grilled Asparagus & Honey-glazed Carrots

Servings: 4
Cooking Time: 35 Minutes
Ingredients:
- 1 bunch asparagus, woody ends removed
- 2 tbsp olive oil
- 1 lb peeled carrots
- 2 tbsp honey
- Sea salt to taste
- Lemon zest to taste

Directions:
1. Rinse the vegetables under cold water.
2. Splash the asparagus with oil and generously with a splash of salt.
3. Drizzle carrots generously with honey and splash lightly with salt.
4. Preheat your to 350F with the lid closed for about 15 minutes.
5. Place the carrots first on the grill and cook for about 10-15 minutes.
6. Now place asparagus on the grill and cook both for about 15-20 minutes or until done to your liking.
7. Top with lemon zest and enjoy.

Nutrition Info: Calories 184, Total fat 7.3g, Saturated fat 1.1g, Total carbs 28.6g, Net carbs 21g, Protein 6g, Sugars 18.5g, Fiber 7.6g, Sodium 142mg, Potassium 826mg

205.   Stuffed Grilled Zucchini

Servings: 4
Cooking Time: 10 Minutes
Ingredients:
- 4 zucchini, medium
- 5 tbsp olive oil, divided
- 2 tbsp red onion, finely chopped
- 1/4 tbsp garlic, minced
- 1/2 cup bread crumbs, dry
- 1/2 cup shredded mozzarella cheese, part-skim
- 1/2 tbsp salt
- 1 tbsp fresh mint, minced
- 3 tbsp parmesan cheese, grated

Directions:
1. Halve zucchini lengthwise and scoop pulp ou. Leave 1/4 -inch shell. Now brush using 2 tbsp oil, set aside, and chop the pulp.
2. Saute onion and pulp in a skillet, large, then add garlic and cook for about 1 minute.
3. Add bread crumbs and cook while stirring for about 2 minutes until golden brown.
4. Remove everything from heat then stir in mozzarella cheese, salt, and mint. Scoop into the zucchini shells and splash with parmesan cheese.
5. Preheat your to 375F.
6. Place stuffed zucchini on the grill and grill while covered for about 8-10 minutes until tender.
7. Serve warm and enjoy.

Nutrition Info: Calories 186, Total fat 10g, Saturated fat 3g, Total carbs 17g, Net carbs 14g, Protein 9g, Sugars 4g, Fiber 3g, Sodium 553mg, Potassium 237mg

206. Grilled Zucchini

Servings: 6
Cooking Time: 10 Minutes
Ingredients:
- 4 medium zucchini
- 2 tablespoons olive oil
- 1 tablespoon sherry vinegar
- 2 sprigs of thyme, leaves chopped
- ½ teaspoon salt
- 1/3 teaspoon ground black pepper

Directions:
1. Switch on the grill, fill the grill hopper with oak flavored wood pellets, power the grill on by using the control panel, select 'smoke' on the temperature dial, or set the temperature to 350 degrees F and let it preheat for a minimum of 5 minutes.
2. Meanwhile, cut the ends of each zucchini, cut each in half and then into thirds and place in a plastic bag.
3. Add remaining ingredients, seal the bag, and shake well to coat zucchini pieces.
4. When the grill has preheated, open the lid, place zucchini on the grill grate, shut the grill and smoke for 4 minutes per side.
5. When done, transfer zucchini to a dish, garnish with more thyme and then serve.
Nutrition Info: Calories: 74 Cal ;Fat: 5.4 g ;Carbs: 6.1 g ;Protein: 2.6 g ;Fiber: 2.3 g

207. Broccoli-cauliflower Salad

Servings: 4
Cooking Time: 25 Minutes
Ingredients:
- 1½ cups mayonnaise
- ½ cup sour cream
- ¼ cup sugar
- 1 bunch broccoli, cut into small pieces
- 1 head cauliflower, cut into small pieces
- 1 small red onion, chopped
- 6 slices bacon, cooked and crumbled (precooked bacon works well)
- 1 cup shredded Cheddar cheese

Directions:
1. In a small bowl, whisk together the mayonnaise, sour cream, and sugar to make a dressing.
2. In a large bowl, combine the broccoli, cauliflower, onion, bacon, and Cheddar cheese.
3. Pour the dressing over the vegetable mixture and toss well to coat.
4. Serve the salad chilled.

208. Wood Pellet Bacon Wrapped Jalapeno Poppers

Servings: 6
Cooking Time: 20 Minutes
Ingredients:
- 6 jalapenos, fresh
- 4 oz cream cheese
- 1/2 cup cheddar cheese, shredded
- 1 tbsp vegetable rub
- 12 slices cut bacon

Directions:
1. Preheat the wood pellet smoker and grill to375°F.
2. Slice the jalapenos lengthwise and scrape the seed and membrane. Rinse them with water and set aside.
3. In a mixing bowl, mix cream cheese, cheddar cheese, vegetable rub until well mixed.
4. Fill the jalapeno halves with the mixture then wrap with the bacon pieces.
5. Smoke for 20 minutes or until the bacon crispy.
6. Serve and enjoy.
Nutrition Info: Calories 1830, Total fat 11g, Saturated fat 6g, Total Carbs 5g, Net Carbs 4g, Protein 6g, Sugar 4g, Fiber 1g

209.   Wood Pellet Grilled Mexican Street Corn

Servings: 6
Cooking Time: 25 Minutes
Ingredients:
- 6 ears of corn on the cob, shucked
- 1 tbsp olive oil
- Kosher salt and pepper to taste
- 1/4 cup mayo
- 1/4 cup sour cream
- 1 tbsp garlic paste
- 1/2 tbsp chili powder
- Pinch of ground red pepper
- 1/2 cup cotija cheese, crumbled
- 1/4 cup cilantro, chopped
- 6 lime wedges

Directions:
1. Brush the corn with oil and sprinkle with salt.
2. Place the corn on a wood pellet grill set at 350°F. Cook for 25 minutes as you turn it occasionally.
3. Meanwhile mix mayo, cream, garlic, chili, and red pepper until well combined.
4. When the corn is cooked remove from the grill, let it rest for some minutes then brush with the mayo mixture.
5. Sprinkle cotija cheese, more chili powder, and cilantro. Serve with lime wedges. Enjoy.

Nutrition Info: Calories 144, Total fat 5g, Saturated fat 2g, Total Carbs 10g, Net Carbs 10g, Protein 0g, Sugar 0g, Fiber 0g, Sodium: 136mg, Potassium 173mg

210.   Grilled Carrots And Asparagus

Servings: 6
Cooking Time: 30 Minutes
Ingredients:
- 1 pound whole carrots, with tops
- 1 bunch of asparagus, ends trimmed
- Sea salt as needed
- 1 teaspoon lemon zest
- 2 tablespoons honey
- 2 tablespoons olive oil

Directions:
1. Switch on the grill, fill the grill hopper with flavored wood pellets, power the grill on by using the control panel, select 'smoke' on the temperature dial, or set the temperature to 450 degrees F and let it preheat for a minimum of 15 minutes.
2. Meanwhile, take a medium dish, place asparagus in it, season with sea salt, drizzle with oil and toss until mixed.
3. Take a medium bowl, place carrots in it, drizzle with honey, sprinkle with sea salt and toss until combined.
4. When the grill has preheated, open the lid, place asparagus and carrots on the grill grate, shut the grill and smoke for 30 minutes.
5. When done, transfer vegetables to a dish, sprinkle with lemon zest, and then serve.

Nutrition Info: Calories: 79.8 Cal ;Fat: 4.8 g ;Carbs: 8.6 g ;Protein: 2.6 g ;Fiber: 3.5 g

211.   Sweet Potato Fries

Servings: 4
Cooking Time: 40 Minutes
Ingredients:
- 3 sweet potatoes, sliced into strips
- 4 tablespoons olive oil
- 2 tablespoons fresh rosemary, chopped
- Salt and pepper to taste

Directions:
1. Set the wood pellet grill to 450 degrees F.
2. Preheat it for 10 minutes.
3. Spread the sweet potato strips in the baking pan.
4. Toss in olive oil and sprinkle with rosemary, salt and pepper.
5. Cook for 15 minutes.
6. Flip and cook for another 15 minutes.
7. Flip and cook for 10 more minutes.
8. Tips: Soak sweet potatoes in water before cooking to prevent browning.

212.   Grilled Baby Carrots And Fennel

Servings: 8
Cooking Time: 30 Minutes
Ingredients:
- 1-pound slender rainbow carrots, washed and peeled
- 2 whole fennel bulbs, chopped
- 2 tablespoons extra virgin olive oil
- 1 teaspoon salt
- Salt to taste

Directions:
1. Fire the Grill to 500F. Use desired wood pellets when cooking. Close the lid and preheat for 15 minutes.
2. Place all ingredients in a sheet tray and toss to coat with oil and seasoning.
3. Place on the grill grate and cook for 30 minutes.

Nutrition Info: Calories per serving:52 ; Protein: 1.2g; Carbs: 8.9g; Fat: 1.7g Sugar: 4.3g

213. Roasted Root Vegetables

Servings: 6
Cooking Time: 45 Minutes
Ingredients:

- 1 large red onion, peeled
- 1 bunch of red beets, trimmed, peeled
- 1 large yam, peeled
- 1 bunch of golden beets, trimmed, peeled
- 1 large parsnips, peeled
- 1 butternut squash, peeled
- 1 large carrot, peeled
- 6 garlic cloves, peeled
- 3 tablespoons thyme leaves
- Salt as needed
- 1 cinnamon stick
- Ground black pepper as needed
- 3 tablespoons olive oil
- 2 tablespoons honey

Directions:
1. Switch on the grill, fill the grill hopper with hickory flavored wood pellets, power the grill on by using the control panel, select 'smoke' on the temperature dial, or set the temperature to 450 degrees F and let it preheat for a minimum of 15 minutes.
2. Meanwhile, cut all the vegetables into ½-inch pieces, place them in a large bowl, add garlic, thyme, and cinnamon, drizzle with oil and toss until mixed.
3. Take a large cookie sheet, line it with foil, spread with vegetables, and then season with salt and black pepper.
4. When the grill has preheated, open the lid, place prepared cookie sheet on the grill grate, shut the grill and smoke for 45 minutes until tender.
5. When done, transfer vegetables to a dish, drizzle with honey, and then serve.

Nutrition Info: Calories: 164 Cal ;Fat: 4 g ;Carbs: 31.7 g ;Protein: 2.7 g ;Fiber: 6.4 g

214. Smoked Baked Kale Chips

Servings: 4
Cooking Time: 30 Minutes
Ingredients:

- 2 bunches kale, stems removed
- Olive oil as needed
- Salt and pepper to taste

Directions:
1. Fire the Grill to 350F. Use desired wood pellets when cooking. Close the lid and preheat for 15 minutes.
2. Place all ingredients in a bowl and toss to coat the kale with oil.
3. Place on a baking tray and spread the leaves evenly on all surface.
4. Place in the grill and cook for 30 minutes or until the kale leaves become crispy.

Nutrition Info: Calories per serving: 206 ; Protein: 9.9g; Carbs: 21g; Fat: 12g Sugar: 0g

215.   Smoked Stuffed Mushrooms

Servings: 12
Cooking Time: 1 Hour 15 Minutes
Ingredients:
- 12-16 white mushrooms, large, cleaned and stems removed
- 1/2 cup parmesan cheese
- 1/2 cup bread crumbs, Italian
- 2 minced garlic cloves
- 2 tbsp fresh parsley, chopped
- 1/4 -1/3 cup olive oil
- Salt and pepper to taste

Directions:
1. Preheat your 375F.
2. Remove mushroom very bottom stem then dice the rest into small pieces.
3. Combine mushroom stems, parmesan cheese, bread crumbs, garlic, parsley, 3 tbsp oil, pepper, and salt in a bowl, large. Combine until moist.
4. Layer mushrooms in a pan, disposable, then fill them with the mixture until heaping. Drizzle with more oil.
5. Place the pan on the grill.
6. Smoke for about 1 hour 20 minutes until filling browns and mushrooms become tender.
7. Remove from and serve.
8. Enjoy!

Nutrition Info: Calories 74, Total fat 6.1g, Saturated fat 1g, Total carbs 4.1g, Net carbs 3.7g, Protein 1.6g, Sugars 0.6g, Fiber 0.4g, Sodium 57mg, Potassium 72mg

216.   Wood Pellet Smoked Vegetables

Servings: 6
Cooking Time: 15 Minutes
Ingredients:
- 1 ear corn, fresh, husks and silk strands removed
- 1yellow squash, sliced
- 1 red onion, cut into wedges
- 1 green pepper, cut into strips
- 1 red pepper, cut into strips
- 1 yellow pepper, cut into strips
- 1 cup mushrooms, halved
- 2 tbsp oil
- 2 tbsp chicken seasoning

Directions:
1. Soak the pecan wood pellets in water for an hour. Remove the pellets from water and fill the smoker box with the wet pellets.
2. Place the smoker box under the grill and close the lid. Heat the grill on high heat for 10 minutes or until smoke starts coming out from the wood chips.
3. Meanwhile, toss the veggies in oil and seasonings then transfer them into a grill basket.
4. Grill for 10 minutes while turning occasionally. Serve and enjoy.

Nutrition Info: Calories 97, Total fat 5g, Saturated fat 2g, Total Carbs 11g, Net Carbs 8g, Protein 2g, Sugar 1g, Fiber 3g, Sodium: 251mg, Potassium 171mg

217. Smoked Deviled Eggs

Servings: 4 To 6
Cooking Time: 50 Minutes
Ingredients:
- 6 large eggs
- 1slice bacon
- 1/4 cup mayonnaise
- 1tsp Dijon mustard
- 1tsp apple cider vinegar
- 1/4 tsp paprika
- Pinch of kosher salt
- 1tbsp chives, chopped

Directions:
1. Preheat pellet grill to 180°F and turn smoke setting on, if applicable.
2. Bring a pot of water to a boil. Add eggs and hard boil eggs for about 12 minutes.
3. Remove eggs from pot and place them into an ice-water bath. Once eggs have cooled completely, peel them and slice in half lengthwise.
4. Place sliced eggs on grill, yolk side up. Smoke for 30 to 45 minutes, depending on how much smoky flavor you want.
5. While eggs smoke, cook bacon until it's crispy.
6. Remove eggs from the grill and allow to cool on a plate.
7. Remove the yolks and place all of them in a small bowl. Place the egg whites on a plate.
8. Mash yolks with a fork and add mayonnaise, mustard, apple cider vinegar, paprika, and salt. Stir until combined.
9. Spoon a scoop of yolk mixture back into each egg white.
10. Sprinkle paprika, chives, and crispy bacon bits to garnish. Serve and enjoy!
Nutrition Info: Calories: 140 Fat: 12 g Cholesterol: 190 mg Carbohydrate: 1 g Fiber: 0 Sugar: 0 Protein: 6 g

218. Vegetable Skewers

Servings: 4
Cooking Time: 20 Minutes
Ingredients:
- 2 cups whole white mushrooms
- 2 large yellow squash, peeled, chopped
- 1 cup chopped pineapple
- 1 cup chopped red pepper
- 1 cup halved strawberries
- 2 large zucchini, chopped
- For the Dressing:
- 2 lemons, juiced
- ½ teaspoon ground black pepper
- 1/2 teaspoon sea salt
- 1 teaspoon red chili powder
- 1 tablespoon maple syrup
- 1 tablespoon orange zest
- 2 tablespoons apple cider vinegar
- 1/4 cup olive oil

Directions:
1. Switch on the grill, fill the grill hopper with flavored wood pellets, power the grill on by using the control panel, select 'smoke' on the temperature dial, or set the temperature to 450 degrees F and let it preheat for a minimum of 5 minutes.
2. Meanwhile, prepared thread vegetables and fruits on skewers alternately and then brush skewers with oil.
3. When the grill has preheated, open the lid, place vegetable skewers on the grill grate, shut the grill, and smoke for 20 minutes until tender and lightly charred.
4. Meanwhile, prepare the dressing and for this, take a small bowl, place all of its ingredients in it and then whisk until combined.
5. When done, transfer skewers to a dish, top with prepared dressing and then serve.
Nutrition Info: Calories: 130 Cal ;Fat: 2 g ;Carbs: 20 g ;Protein: 2 g ;Fiber: 0.3 g

219.   Salt-crusted Baked Potatoes

Servings: 6
Cooking Time: 40 Minutes
Ingredients:
- 6 russet potatoes, scrubbed and dried
- 3 tablespoons oil
- 1 tablespoons salt
- Butter as needed
- Sour cream as needed

Directions:
1. Fire the Grill to 400F. Use desired wood pellets when cooking. Close the lid and preheat for 15 minutes.
2. In a large bowl, coat the potatoes with oil and salt. Place seasoned potatoes on a baking tray.
3. Place the tray with potatoes on the grill grate.
4. Close the lid and grill for 40 minutes.
5. Serve with butter and sour cream.

Nutrition Info: Calories per serving: 363; Protein: 8g; Carbs: 66.8g; Fat: 8.6g Sugar: 2.3g

220.   Minestrone Soup

Servings: 4
Cooking Time: 35 Minutes
Ingredients:
- 1/4 tsp. Black Pepper
- 2tbsp. Olive Oil
- 15 oz. Cannellini Beans
- 1Onion quartered
- 1/2 tsp. Salt
- 2Garlic cloves, minced
- 1/3 cup Parmesan Cheese, grated
- 2Rosemary sprigs, minced
- 1cup Kale leaves, chopped
- 4cups Vegetable Stock
- Juice and Zest of 1 Lemon

Directions:
1. Begin by keeping oil, onion, and garlic in the pitcher of the blender.
2. Next, select the 'saute' button.
3. Once sautéed, stir in celery, rosemary, vegetable stock, lemon zest, lemon juice, kale, parmesan, salt, and pepper.
4. Then, press the 'hearty soup' button.
5. When it takes only 5 to 6 minutes to finish, add the beans and continue cooking.

Nutrition Info: Calories: 34 Fat: 1 g Total Carbs: 4.7 g Fiber: 0.4 g Sugar: 0 g Protein: 1.8 g Cholesterol: 1 mg

221.   Shiitake Smoked Mushrooms

Servings: 4-6
Cooking Time: 45 Minutes
Ingredients:
- 4 Cup Shiitake Mushrooms
- 1 tbsp canola oil
- 1 tsp onion powder
- 1 tsp granulated garlic
- 1 tsp salt
- 1 tsp pepper

Directions:
1. Combine all the ingredients together
2. Apply the mix over the mushrooms generously.
3. Preheat the smoker at 180°F. Add wood chips and half a bowl of water in the side tray.
4. Place it in the smoker and smoke for 45 minutes.
5. Serve warm and enjoy.

Nutrition Info: Calories: 301 Cal Fat: 9 g Carbohydrates: 47.8 g   Protein: 7.1 g Fiber: 4.8 g

222. Grilled Artichokes

Servings: 6
Cooking Time: 15 Minutes
Ingredients:
- 3 large artichokes, blanched and halved
- 3 + 3 tablespoons olive oil
- Salt and pepper to taste
- 1 cup mayonnaise
- 1 cup yogurt
- 2 tablespoons parsley, chopped
- 2 tablespoons capers
- Lemon juice to taste

Directions:
1. Fire the Grill to 500F. Use desired wood pellets when cooking. Close the lid and preheat for 15 minutes.
2. Brush the artichokes with 3 tablespoons of olive oil. Season with salt and pepper to taste.
3. Place on the grill grate and cook for 15 minutes.
4. Allow to cool before slicing.
5. Once cooled, slice the artichokes and place in a bowl.
6. In another bowl, mix together the mayonnaise, yogurt, parsley, capers, and lemon juice. Season with salt and pepper to taste. Mix until well-combined.
7. Pour sauce over the artichokes.
8. Toss to coat.

Nutrition Info: Calories per serving: 257; Protein: 6.7g; Carbs: 13.2 g; Fat: 20.9g Sugar: 3.7g

223. Grilled Potato Salad

Servings: 8
Cooking Time: 10 Minutes
Ingredients:
- 1 ½ pound fingerling potatoes, halved lengthwise
- 1 small jalapeno, sliced
- 10 scallions
- 2 teaspoons salt
- 2 tablespoons rice vinegar
- 2 teaspoons lemon juice
- 2/3 cup olive oil, divided

Directions:
1. Switch on the grill, fill the grill hopper with pecan flavored wood pellets, power the grill on by using the control panel, select 'smoke' on the temperature dial, or set the temperature to 450 degrees F and let it preheat for a minimum of 5 minutes.
2. Meanwhile, prepare scallions, and for this, brush them with some oil.
3. When the grill has preheated, open the lid, place scallions on the grill grate, shut the grill and smoke for 3 minutes until lightly charred.
4. Then transfer scallions to a cutting board, let them cool for 5 minutes, then cut into slices and set aside until required.
5. Brush potatoes with some oil, season with some salt and black pepper, place potatoes on the grill grate, shut the grill and smoke for 5 minutes until thoroughly cooked.
6. Then take a large bowl, pour in remaining oil, add salt, lemon juice, and vinegar and stir until combined.
7. Add grilled scallion and potatoes, toss until well mixed, taste to adjust seasoning and then serve.

Nutrition Info: Calories: 223.7 Cal ;Fat: 12 g ;Carbs: 27 g ;Protein: 1.9 g ;Fiber: 3.3 g

224.   Wood Pellet Smoked Acorn Squash

Servings: 6
Cooking Time: 2 Hours
Ingredients:
- 3 tbsp olive oil
- 3 acorn squash, halved and seeded
- 1/4 cup unsalted butter
- 1/4 cup brown sugar
- 1 tbsp cinnamon, ground
- 1 tbsp chili powder
- 1 tbsp nutmeg, ground

Directions:
1. Brush olive oil on the acorn squash cut sides then cover the halves with foil. Poke holes on the foil to allow steam and smoke through.
2. Fire up the wood pellet to 225°F and smoke the squash for 1-1/2-2 hours.
3. Remove the squash from the smoker and allow it to sit.
4. Meanwhile, melt butter, sugar and spices in a saucepan. Stir well to combine.
5. Remove the foil from the squash and spoon the butter mixture in each squash half. Enjoy.

Nutrition Info: Calories 149, Total fat 10g, Saturated fat 5g, Total Carbs 14g, Net Carbs 12g, Protein 2g, Sugar 0g, Fiber 2g, Sodium: 19mg, Potassium 0mg

225.   Kale Chips

Servings: 6
Cooking Time: 20 Minutes
Ingredients:
- 2 bunches of kale, stems removed
- ½ teaspoon of sea salt
- 4 tablespoons olive oil

Directions:
1. Switch on the grill, fill the grill hopper with apple-flavored wood pellets, power the grill on by using the control panel, select 'smoke' on the temperature dial, or set the temperature to 250 degrees F and let it preheat for a minimum of 15 minutes.
2. Meanwhile, rinse the kale leaves, pat dry, spread the kale on a sheet tray, drizzle with oil, season with salt and toss until well coated.
3. When the grill has preheated, open the lid, place sheet tray on the grill grate, shut the grill and smoke for 20 minutes until crisp.
4. Serve straight away.

Nutrition Info: Calories: 110 Cal ;Fat: 5 g ;Carbs: 15.8 g ;Protein: 5.3 g ;Fiber: 5.6 g

226.   Smoked Acorn Squash

Servings: 6
Cooking Time: 2 Hours
Ingredients:
- 3 acorn squash, seeded and halved
- 3 tbsp olive oil
- 1/4 cup butter, unsalted
- 1 tbsp cinnamon, ground
- 1 tbsp chili powder
- 1 tbsp nutmeg, ground
- 1/4 cup brown sugar

Directions:
1. Brush the cut sides of your squash with olive oil then cover with foil poking holes for smoke and steam to get through.
2. Preheat your to 225F.
3. Place the squash halves on the grill with the cut side down and smoke for about 1½- 2 hours. Remove from the Traeger.
4. Let it sit while you prepare spiced butter. Melt butter in a saucepan then add spices and sugar stirring to combine.
5. Remove the foil form the squash halves.
6. Place 1 tbsp of the butter mixture onto each half.
7. Serve and enjoy!

Nutrition Info: Calories 149, Total 10g, Saturated fat 5g, Total carbs 14g, Net carbs 12g, Protein 2g, Sugars 2g, Fiber 2g, Sodium 19mg, Potassium 101m

227. Blt Pasta Salad

Servings: 6
Cooking Time: 35 To 45 Minutes
Ingredients:
- 1 pound thick-cut bacon
- 16 ounces bowtie pasta, cooked according to package directions and drained
- 2 tomatoes, chopped
- ½ cup chopped scallions
- ½ cup Italian dressing
- ½ cup ranch dressing
- 1 tablespoon chopped fresh basil
- 1 teaspoon salt
- 1 teaspoon freshly ground black pepper
- 1 teaspoon garlic powder
- 1 head lettuce, cored and torn

Directions:
1. Supply your smoker with wood pellets and follow the manufacturer's specific start-up procedure. Preheat, with the lid closed, to 225°F.
2. Arrange the bacon slices on the grill grate, close the lid, and cook for 30 to 45 minutes, flipping after 20 minutes, until crisp.
3. Remove the bacon from the grill and chop.
4. In a large bowl, combine the chopped bacon with the cooked pasta, tomatoes, scallions, Italian dressing, ranch dressing, basil, salt, pepper, and garlic powder. Refrigerate until ready to serve.
5. Toss in the lettuce just before serving to keep it from wilting.

228. Grilled Sweet Potato Planks

Servings: 8
Cooking Time: 30 Minutes
Ingredients:
- 5 sweet potatoes, sliced into planks
- 1 tablespoon olive oil
- 1 teaspoon onion powder
- Salt and pepper to taste

Directions:
1. Set the wood pellet grill to high.
2. Preheat it for 15 minutes while the lid is closed.
3. Coat the sweet potatoes with oil.
4. Sprinkle with onion powder, salt and pepper.
5. Grill the sweet potatoes for 15 minutes.
6. Tips: Grill for a few more minutes if you want your sweet potatoes crispier.

229.   Smoked Pumpkin Soup

Servings: 6
Cooking Time: 1 Hour And 33 Minutes
Ingredients:
- 5 pounds pumpkin, seeded and sliced
- 3 tablespoons butter
- 1 onion, diced
- 2 cloves garlic, minced
- 1 tablespoon brown sugar
- 1 teaspoon paprika
- ¼ teaspoon ground cinnamon
- ¼ teaspoon ground nutmeg
- ½ cup apple cider
- 5 cups broth
- ½ cup cream

Directions:
1. Fire the Grill to 180F. Use desired wood pellets when cooking. Close the lid and preheat for 15 minutes.
2. Place the pumpkin on the grill grate and smoke for an hour or until tender. Allow to cool.
3. Melt the butter in a large saucepan over medium heat and sauté the onion and garlic for 3 minutes. Stir in the rest of the ingredients including the smoked pumpkin. Cook for another 30 minutes.
4. Transfer to a blender and pulse until smooth.

Nutrition Info: Calories per serving: 246; Protein: 8.8g; Carbs: 32.2g; Fat: 11.4g Sugar: 15.5g

230.   Chicken Tortilla Soup

Servings: 4
Cooking Time: 35 Minutes
Ingredients:
- 1/2 cup Black Beans, canned
- 1Jalapeno Pepper, halved and seeds removed
- 1-1/2 cup Chicken Stock
- 2Carrots, sliced into ¼-inch pieces
- 1/2 of 1 Onion, peeled and halved
- 1/2 cup Corn
- 3 Garlic cloves
- 14-1/2 oz. Fire Roasted Tomatoes
- 1/4 cup Cilantro Leaves
- 10 oz. Chicken Breast, diced into ½ inch
- For the seasoning mix:
- 1/4 tsp. Chipotle
- 1tsp. Cuminutes
- 1/2 tsp. Sea Salt
- 1/2 tsp. Smoked Paprika

Directions:
1. Place pepper, carrots, onion, garlic cloves, and cilantro in the blender pitcher.
2. Pulse the mixture for 3 minutes and then pour the chicken stock to it.
3. Pulse again for another 3 minutes.
4. Next, stir in the remaining ingredients and press the 'hearty soup' button.
5. Finally, transfer to the serving bowl.

Nutrition Info: Calories: 260 Fat: 4 g Total Carbs: 40 g Fiber: 5.9 g Sugar: 8 g Protein: 14 g Cholesterol: 20 mg

231.   Roasted Veggies & Hummus

Servings: 4
Cooking Time: 20 Minutes
Ingredients:
- 1 white onion, sliced into wedges
- 2 cups butternut squash
- 2 cups cauliflower, sliced into florets
- 1 cup mushroom buttons
- Olive oil
- Salt and pepper to taste
- Hummus

Directions:
1. Set the wood pellet grill to high.
2. Preheat it for 10 minutes while the lid is closed.
3. Add the veggies to a baking pan.
4. Roast for 20 minutes.
5. Serve roasted veggies with hummus.
6. Tips: You can also spread a little hummus on the vegetables before roasting.

232.   Roasted Vegetable Medley

Servings: 4 To 6
Cooking Time: 50 Minutes
Ingredients:
- 2medium potatoes, cut to 1 inch wedges
- 2red bell peppers, cut into 1 inch cubes
- 1small butternut squash, peeled and cubed to 1 inch cube
- 1red onion, cut to 1 inch cubes
- 1cup broccoli, trimmed
- 2tbsp olive oil
- 1tbsp balsamic vinegar
- 1tbsp fresh rosemary, minced
- 1tbsp fresh thyme, minced
- 1tsp kosher salt
- 1tsp ground black pepper

Directions:
1. Preheat pellet grill to 425°F.
2. In a large bowl, combine potatoes, peppers, squash, and onion.
3. In a small bowl, whisk together olive oil, balsamic vinegar, rosemary, thyme, salt, and pepper.
4. Pour marinade over vegetables and toss to coat. Allow resting for about 15 minutes.
5. Place marinated vegetables into a grill basket, and place a grill basket on the grill grate. Cook for about 30-40 minutes, occasionally tossing in the grill basket.
6. Remove veggies from grill and transfer to a serving dish. Allow to cool for 5 minutes, then serve and enjoy!

Nutrition Info: Calories: 158.6 Fat: 7.4 g Cholesterol: 0 Carbohydrate: 22 g Fiber: 7.2 g Sugar: 3.1 g Protein: 5.2 g

233.   Wood Pellet Grilled Zucchini Squash Spears

Servings: 5
Cooking Time: 10 Minutes
Ingredients:
- 4 zucchini, cleaned and ends cut
- 2 tbsp olive oil
- 1 tbsp sherry vinegar
- 2 thyme, leaves pulled
- Salt and pepper to taste

Directions:
1. Cut the zucchini into halves then cut each half thirds.
2. Add the rest of the ingredients in a ziplock bag with the zucchini pieces. Toss to mix well.
3. Preheat the wood pellet temperature to 350°F with the lid closed for 15 minutes.
4. Remove the zucchini from the bag and place them on the grill grate with the cut side down.
5. Cook for 4 minutes per side or until the zucchini are tender.
6. Remove from grill and serve with thyme leaves. Enjoy.

Nutrition Info: Calories 74, Total fat 5.4g, Saturated fat 0.5g, Total Carbs 6.1g, Net Carbs 3.8g, Protein 2.6g, Sugar 3.9g, Fiber 2.3g, Sodium: 302mg, Potassium 599mg

234.   Grilled Broccoli

Servings: 1-2
Cooking Time: 3 Minutes
Ingredients:
- 2cups of broccoli, fresh
- 1tablespoon of canola oil
- 1teaspoon of lemon pepper

Directions:
1. Place the grill; grate inside the unit and close the hood.
2. Preheat the grill by turning at high for 10 minutes.
3. Meanwhile, mix broccoli with lemon pepper and canola oil.
4. Toss well to coat the Ingredients: thoroughly.
5. Place it on a grill grade once add food appears.
6. Lock the unit and cook for 3 minutes at medium.
7. Take out and serve.

Nutrition Info: Calories: 96 Total Fat: 7.3g Saturated Fat: 0.5g Cholesterol: 0mg Sodium: 30mg Total Carbohydrate: 6.7g Dietary Fiber 2.7g Total Sugars: 1.6g Protein: 2.7g

235.   Green Beans With Bacon

Servings: 6
Cooking Time: 20 Minutes
Ingredients:
- 4 strips of bacon, chopped
- 1 1/2 pound green beans, ends trimmed
- 1 teaspoon minced garlic
- 1 teaspoon salt
- 4 tablespoons olive oil

Directions:
1. Switch on the grill, fill the grill hopper with flavored wood pellets, power the grill on by using the control panel, select 'smoke' on the temperature dial, or set the temperature to 450 degrees F and let it preheat for a minimum of 15 minutes.
2. Meanwhile, take a sheet tray, place all the ingredients in it and toss until mixed.
3. When the grill has preheated, open the lid, place prepared sheet tray on the grill grate, shut the grill and smoke for 20 minutes until lightly browned and cooked.
4. When done, transfer green beans to a dish and then serve.

Nutrition Info: Calories: 93 Cal ;Fat: 4.6 g ;Carbs: 8.2 g ;Protein: 5.9 g ;Fiber: 2.9 g

236. Grilled Romaine Caesar Salad

Servings: 6
Cooking Time: 5 Minutes
Ingredients:
- ¼ cup extra virgin olive oil
- 2 cloves garlic, minced
- 1 teaspoon Dijon mustard
- 1 cup mayonnaise
- Salt and pepper to taste
- 2 head Romaine lettuce
- ¼ cup parmesan cheese
- Croutons, optional

Directions:
1. In a small bowl, combine the olive oil, garlic, mustard, and mayonnaise. Season with salt and pepper to taste. Mix and set aside.
2. Cut the Romaine in half lengthwise leaving the ends intact so that it does not come apart.
3. Fire the Grill to 400F. Use desired wood pellets when cooking. Close the lid and preheat for 15 minutes.
4. Brush the Romaine lettuce with oil and place cut side down on the grill grate. Cook for 5 minutes.
5. Once cooked, chop the lettuce and place on a bowl. Toss with the salad dressing, parmesan cheese, and croutons.

Nutrition Info: Calories per serving: 235 ; Protein: 7.5g; Carbs: 19.4 g; Fat: 9.7g Sugar: 8.3g

237. Bunny Dogs With Sweet And Spicy Jalapeño Relish

Servings: 8
Cooking Time: 35 To 40 Minutes
Ingredients:
- 8 hot dog-size carrots, peeled
- ¼ cup honey
- ¼ cup yellow mustard
- Nonstick cooking spray or butter, for greasing
- Salt
- Freshly ground black pepper
- 8 hot dog buns
- Sweet and Spicy Jalapeño Relish

Directions:
1. Prepare the carrots by removing the stems and slicing in half lengthwise.
2. In a small bowl, whisk together the honey and mustard.
3. Supply your smoker with wood pellets and follow the manufacturer's specific start-up procedure. Preheat, with the lid closed, to 375°F.
4. Line a baking sheet with aluminum foil and coat with cooking spray.
5. Brush the carrots on both sides with the honey mustard and season with salt and pepper; put on the baking sheet.
6. Place the baking sheet on the grill grate, close the lid, and smoke for 35 to 40 minutes, or until tender and starting to brown.
7. To serve, lightly toast the hot dog buns on the grill and top each with two slices of carrot and some relish.

238. Roasted Butternut Squash

Servings: 4
Cooking Time: 30 Minutes
Ingredients:
- 2-pound butternut squash
- 3 tablespoon extra-virgin olive oil
- Veggie Rub, as needed

Directions:
1. Fire the Grill to 350F. Use desired wood pellets when cooking. Close the lid and preheat for 15 minutes.
2. Slice the butternut squash into ½ inch thick and remove the seeds. Season with oil and veggie rub.
3. Place the seasoned squash in a baking tray.
4. Grill for 30 minutes.

Nutrition Info: Calories per serving: 131; Protein: 1.9g; Carbs: 23.6g; Fat: 4.7g Sugar: 0g

239. Baked Cheesy Corn Pudding

Servings: 6
Cooking Time: 30 Minutes
Ingredients:
- 3 cloves of garlic, chopped
- 3 tablespoons butter
- 3 cups whole corn kernels
- 8 ounces cream cheese
- 1 cup cheddar cheese
- 1 cup parmesan cheese
- 1 tablespoon salt
- ½ tablespoon black pepper
- ½ cup dry breadcrumbs
- 1 cup mozzarella cheese, grated
- 1 tablespoon thyme, minced

Directions:
1. Fire the Grill to 350F. Use desired wood pellets when cooking. Close the lid and preheat for 15 minutes.
2. In a large saucepan, sauté the garlic and butter for 2 minutes until fragrant. Add the corn, cheddar cheese, parmesan cheese, salt, and pepper. Heat until the corn is melted then pour into a baking dish.
3. In a small bowl, combine the breadcrumbs, mozzarella cheese, and thyme.
4. Spread the cheese and bread crumb mixture on top of the corn mixture.
5. Place the baking dish on the grill grate and cook for 25 minutes.
6. Allow to rest before removing from the mold.

Nutrition Info: Calories per serving: 523; Protein: 29.4g; Carbs: 34g; Fat: 31.2g Sugar: 10.8g

240. Smoked Hummus

Servings: 6
Cooking Time: 20 Minutes
Ingredients:
- 1 ½ cups chickpeas, rinsed and drained
- ¼ cup tahini
- 1 tablespoon garlic, minced
- 2 tablespoons extra virgin olive oil
- 1 teaspoon salt
- 4 tablespoons lemon juice

Directions:
1. Fire the Grill to 350F. Use desired wood pellets when cooking. Close the lid and preheat for 15 minutes.
2. Spread the chickpeas on a sheet tray and place on the grill grate. Smoke for 20 minutes.
3. Let the chickpeas cool at room temperature.
4. Place smoked chickpeas in a blender or food processor. Add in the rest of the ingredients. Pulse until smooth.
5. Serve with roasted vegetables if desired.

Nutrition Info: Calories per serving: 271; Protein: 12.1g; Carbs: 34.8g; Fat: 10.4g Sugar: 5.7g

241.   Easy Smoked Vegetables

Servings: 6
Cooking Time: 1 ½ Hour
Ingredients:
- 1 cup of pecan wood chips
- 1 ear fresh corn, silk strands removed, and husks, cut corn into 1-inch pieces
- 1 medium yellow squash, 1/2-inch slices
- 1 small red onion, thin wedges
- 1 small green bell pepper, 1-inch strips
- 1 small red bell pepper, 1-inch strips
- 1 small yellow bell pepper, 1-inch strips
- 1 cup mushrooms, halved
- 2 tbsp vegetable oil
- Vegetable seasonings

Directions:
1. Take a large bowl and toss all the vegetables together in it. Sprinkle it with seasoning and coat all the vegetables well with it.
2. Place the wood chips and a bowl of water in the smoker.
3. Preheat the smoker at 100°F or ten minutes.
4. Put the vegetables in a pan and add to the middle rack of the electric smoker.
5. Smoke for thirty minutes until the vegetable becomes tender.
6. When done, serve, and enjoy.

Nutrition Info: Calories: 97 Cal Fat: 5 g Carbohydrates: 11 g   Protein: 2 g Fiber: 3 g

242.   Wood Pellet Grill Spicy Sweet Potatoes

Servings: 6
Cooking Time: 35 Minutes
Ingredients:
- 2 lb sweet potatoes, cut into chunks
- 1 red onion, chopped
- 2 tbsp oil
- 2 tbsp orange juice
- 1 tbsp roasted cinnamon
- 1 tbsp salt
- 1/4 tbsp Chiptole chili pepper

Directions:
1. Preheat the wood pellet grill to 425°F with the lid closed.
2. Toss the sweet potatoes with onion, oil, and juice.
3. In a mixing bowl, mix cinnamon, salt, and pepper then sprinkle the mixture over the sweet potatoes.
4. Spread the potatoes on a lined baking dish in a single layer.
5. Place the baking dish in the grill and grill for 30 minutes or until the sweet potatoes ate tender.
6. Serve and enjoy.

Nutrition Info: Calories 145, Total fat 5g, Saturated fat 0g, Total Carbs 23g, Net Carbs 19g, Protein 2g, Sugar 3g, Fiber 4g, Sodium: 428mg, Potassium 230mg

243. Smoked Potato Salad

Servings: 4
Cooking Time: 40 Minutes
Ingredients:
- 2 lb. potatoes
- 2 tablespoons olive oil
- 2 cups mayonnaise
- 1 tablespoon white wine vinegar
- 1 tablespoon dry mustard
- 1/2 onion, chopped
- 2 celery stalks, chopped
- Salt and pepper to taste

Directions:
1. Coat the potatoes with oil.
2. Smoke the potatoes in the wood pellet grill at 180 degrees F for 20 minutes.
3. Increase temperature to 450 degrees F and cook for 20 more minutes.
4. Transfer to a bowl and let cool.
5. Peel potatoes.
6. Slice into cubes.
7. Refrigerate for 30 minutes.
8. Stir in the rest of the ingredients.
9. Tips: You can also add chopped hard-boiled eggs to the mixture.

244. Carolina Baked Beans

Servings: 12 To 15 Minutes
Cooking Time: 2 To 3 Hours
Ingredients:
- 3 (28-ounce) cans baked beans (I like Bush's brand)
- 1 large onion, finely chopped
- 1 cup The Ultimate BBQ Sauce
- ½ cup light brown sugar
- ¼ cup Worcestershire sauce
- 3 tablespoons yellow mustard
- Nonstick cooking spray or butter, for greasing
- 1 large bell pepper, cut into thin rings
- ½ pound thick-cut bacon, partially cooked and cut into quarters

Directions:
1. Supply your smoker with wood pellets and follow the manufacturer's specific start-up procedure. Preheat, with the lid closed, to 300°F.
2. In a large mixing bowl, stir together the beans, onion, barbecue sauce, brown sugar, Worcestershire sauce, and mustard until well combined
3. Coat a 9-by-13-inch aluminum pan with cooking spray or butter.
4. Pour the beans into the pan and top with the bell pepper rings and bacon pieces, pressing them down slightly into the sauce.
5. Place a layer of heavy-duty foil on the grill grate to catch drips, and place the pan on top of the foil. Close the lid and cook for 2 hours 30 minutes to 3 hours, or until the beans are hot, thick, and bubbly.
6. Let the beans rest for 5 minutes before serving.

245.   Crispy Maple Bacon Brussels Sprouts

Servings: 6
Cooking Time: 1 Hour
Ingredients:
- 1lb brussels sprouts, trimmed and quartered
- 6 slices thick-cut bacon
- 3tbsp maple syrup
- 1tsp olive oil
- 1/2 tsp kosher salt
- 1/2 tsp ground black pepper

Directions:
1. Preheat pellet grill to 425°F.
2. Cut bacon into 1/2 inch thick slices.
3. Place brussels sprouts in a single layer in the cast iron skillet. Drizzle with olive oil and maple syrup, then toss to coat. Sprinkle bacon slices on top then season with kosher salt and black pepper.
4. Place skillet in the pellet grill and roast for about 40 to 45 minutes, or until the brussels sprouts are caramelized and brown.
5. Remove skillet from grill and allow brussels sprouts to cool for about 5 to 10 minutes. Serve and enjoy!

Nutrition Info: Calories: 175.3 Fat: 12.1 g Cholesterol: 6.6 mg Carbohydrate: 13.6 g Fiber: 2.9 g Sugar: 7.6 g Protein: 4.8 g

246.   Roasted Peach Salsa

Servings: 6
Cooking Time: 10 Minutes
Ingredients:
- 6 whole peaches, pitted and halved
- 3 tomatoes, chopped
- 2 whole onions, chopped
- ½ cup cilantro, chopped
- 2 cloves garlic, minced
- 5 teaspoons apple cider vinegar
- ½ teaspoon salt
- ¼ teaspoon black pepper
- 2 tablespoons olive oil

Directions:
1. Fire the Grill to 300F. Use desired wood pellets when cooking. Close the lid and preheat for 15 minutes.
2. Place the peaches on the grill grate and cook for 5 minutes on each side. Remove from the grill and allow to rest for 5 minutes.
3. Place the peaches, tomatoes, onion, and cilantro in a salad bowl. On a smaller bowl, stir in the garlic, apple cider vinegar, salt, pepper, and olive oil. Stir until well-combined. Pour into the salad and toss to coat.

Nutrition Info: Calories per serving: 155 ; Protein: 3.1g; Carbs: 27.6 g; Fat: 5.1g Sugar: 20g

247. Smoked Healthy Cabbage

Servings: 5
Cooking Time: 2 Hours
Ingredients:
- 1head cabbage, cored
- 4tablespoons butter
- 2tablespoons rendered bacon fat
- 1chicken bouillon cube
- 1teaspoon fresh ground black pepper
- 1garlic clove, minced

Directions:
1. Preheat your smoker to 240 degrees Fahrenheit using your preferred wood
2. Fill the hole of your cored cabbage with butter, bouillon cube, bacon fat, pepper and garlic
3. Wrap the cabbage in foil about two-thirds of the way up
4. Make sure to leave the top open
5. Transfer to your smoker rack and smoke for 2 hours
6. Unwrap and enjoy!

Nutrition Info: Calories: 231 Fats: 10g Carbs: 26g Fiber: 1g

248. Grilled Zucchini Squash Spears

Servings: 4
Cooking Time: 10 Minutes
Ingredients:
- 4 zucchini, medium
- 2 tbsp olive oil
- 1 tbsp sherry vinegar
- 2 thyme, leaves pulled
- Salt to taste
- Pepper to taste

Directions:
1. Clean zucchini, cut ends off, half each lengthwise, and cut each half into thirds.
2. Combine all the other ingredients in a zip lock bag, medium, then add spears.
3. Toss well and mix to coat the zucchini.
4. Preheat to 350F with the lid closed for about 15 minutes.
5. Remove spears from the zip lock bag and place them directly on your grill grate with the cut side down.
6. Cook for about 3-4 minutes until zucchini is tender and grill marks show.
7. Remove them from the grill and enjoy.

Nutrition Info: Calories 93, Total fat 7.4g, Saturated fat 1.1g, Total carbs 7.1g, Net carbs 4.9g, Protein 2.4g, Sugars 3.4g, Fiber 2.2g, Sodium 59mg, Potassium 515mg

249.   Smoked Mushrooms

Servings: 2
Cooking Time: 45 Minutes
Ingredients:
- 4 cups whole baby portobello, cleaned
- 1 tbsp canola oil
- 1 tbsp onion powder
- 1 tbsp garlic, granulated
- 1 tbsp salt
- 1 tbsp pepper

Directions:
1. Place all the ingredients in a bowl, mix, and combine.
2. Set your to 180F.
3. Place the mushrooms on the grill directly and smoke for about 30 minutes.
4. Increase heat to high and cook the mushroom for another 15 minutes.
5. Serve warm and enjoy!

Nutrition Info: Calories 118, Total fat 7.6g, Saturated fat 0.6g, Total carbs 10.8g, Net carbs 8.3g, Protein 5.4g, Sugars 3.7g, Fiber 2.5g, Sodium 3500mg, Potassium 536mg

250.   Spinach Soup

Servings: 4
Cooking Time: 35 Minutes
Ingredients:
- 2cups Chicken Stock
- 2tbsp. Vegetable Oil
- 1Onion quartered
- 2 ½ cup Spinach
- ½ lb. Red Potatoes, sliced thinly
- 2cups Milk, whole
- 1Leek, large and sliced thinly
- Black Pepper and Sea Salt, as needed
- 1Thyme Sprigs
- 1Bay Leaf

Directions:
1. For making this healthy soup, place the oil, onion, bay leaf, and thyme in the blender pitcher.
2. Now, press the 'saute' button.
3. Once sautéed, stir in the rest of the ingredients and press the 'smooth soup' button.
4. Finally, transfer the soup to the serving bowls and serve it hot.

Nutrition Info: Calories: 403 Fat: 24 g Total Carbs: 32 g Fiber: 3 g Sugar: 5.5 g Protein: 15 g Cholesterol: 66 mg

CPSIA information can be obtained
at www.ICGtesting.com
Printed in the USA
BVHW050832220221
600778BV00010B/1226

9 781801 248242